Public Participation in Local School Districts

Lexington Books Politics of Education Series
Frederick M. Wirt, Editor

Public Participation in Local School Districts

The Dissatisfaction Theory of Democracy

Edited by

Frank W. Lutz
The Pennsylvania State University

Laurence Iannaccone
University of California

Lexington Books
D.C. Heath and Company
Lexington, Massachusetts
Toronto

Library of Congress Cataloging in Publication Data

Main entry under title:
Public participation in local school districts.

1. School districts—United States—Addresses, essays, lectures. 2. Citizen advisory committees in education—Addresses, essays, lectures. I. Lutz, Frank W. II. Iannoccone, Laurence.
LB2817.P8   379'.1535'0973   77-260
ISBN 0-669-01466-4

Published simultaneously in Canada.

Printed in the United States of America.

International Standard Book Number: 0-669-01466-4

Library of Congress Catalog Card Number: 77-260

Contents

Unsigned chapters were coauthored by the editors of this book.

Preface

The purpose of this preface is to place the following chapters in a context of research, theory, and practice in educational administration. In this way we will demonstrate that the rational process of research is not separated from practice and practical reality in education. We will demonstrate that research and practice are inextricably interrelated, each advancing the other, as the right leg advances the left leg but then must pause to allow the left to advance the right. Only in this way do "we" make smooth progress, together, not separately. The alternative is a sporatic, segmented, and halting-hopping that balances precariously at best and usually falls of its own weight.

The Beginning of a Line of Inquiry

The Midwestern school district of Robertsdale was in a state of unresolved conflict during the late 1950s. This resulted in a school board incumbent defeat in that district in 1960. Through a chain of fortuitous circumstances, this incumbent defeat provided the opportunity to conduct a study which resulted in an ethnographic description of a local school board, which has become known as "the Robertsdale case."[1]

The Ethnographic Study

By the participant/observer method of the field ethnographer and with the guidance of a set of tentatively held but theoretically derived assumptions (or statements), field observations were made for a 3-year period. The original assumptions were derived from small-group theoretical positions and were structured on the generalized assumption that a school board operated as a social system within a larger social system, or macrosystem.

The data included the usual participant/observer diary (observations and informant data). It included historical as well as other data available from public records such as minutes, newspaper articles, and official records of the school district and the state. All these data were organized and used to verify, modify, or reformulate the original assumptions. Restated assumptions were combined so as to provide an explanatory model of school board member incumbent defeat and superintendent turnover.

The Explanatory Model

The explanatory model developed from the Robertsdale case was the type of model described by Caws.[2] It was the result of synthesizing the operational model (observed by the researcher) and the representational model (in the minds of the natives). It identified the important and recurring variables. It was not only what occurred empirically or what was perceived phenomenologically but rather the relationship between those two models that produced certain results under specified conditions. The statements in the model described the data collected over a 3-year period. Although not hypotheses, the statements could be expressed in hypothetical form. As such, they represented a step in theory building, and they were representative of the type of "grounded theory" referred to by Glasser and Strauss.[3] Hypotheses from grounded theory are derived from careful empirical observation as opposed to armchair meditation.

Placing the Model in Cultural Context

Explicit in the explanatory model is the notion that school boards operate as subsystems in a larger macrosystem—the community or school district. Implicit in the model is the concept that the school board has a culture of its own as well as interacting in the larger cultural system of the community, the state, and the nation. Essential to the theory that will be developed in this book is an understanding of culture, its role in the change, and the persistence of organizations within it. In chapter 1 Ramsey develops a general model of conflict and culture in broad anthropological terms, pointing to conditions that have lead to the present stage of educational anthropology. Chapter 2 posits a more specific model of school boards in culture and conflict.

Verification Studies

Based on the original explanatory model, three verification studies were undertaken in California. Each developed statistically testable hypotheses from the model. Each developed operational measures of the variables indicated in the model as well as a statistical design to determine whether the relationship among the variables could be demonstrated. One study tested the relationship between selected economic, social, and political variables and school board incumbent defeat.[4] Another tested the relationship between school board member incumbent defeat and involuntary superintendent turnover.[5] In these studies, statistically significant relationships were demonstrated. The third piece of research investigated the relationship between incumbent defeat (and its assumed relation to change) and the succession of outsider superintendents.[6] These studies will be reported by Walden in chapter 3. Together they seemed to verify the explanatory model.

Additional Verification

All the above studies, as well as the ethnographic study which developed the original explanatory model, were done in school districts where school board members were elected on nonpartisan tickets. The question remained: Do political parties affect the occurrence of incumbent school board member defeat in such a way as to affect the relationship between that variable and the superintendent's tenure? Put another way, if the relationship between school board member incumbent defeat and involuntary superintendent turnover was so strong, could the intervention of party politics into the election (at least so far as having Republicans run against Democrats for school board seats) upset this relationship? This question was investigated by Moen.[7] Several interesting relationships between party membership and incumbent school board member election or defeat were evidenced, but a relationship significantly beyond the .01 level between incumbent defeat in partisan elections and involuntary superintendent turnover was demonstrated, further strengthening the explanatory model. That research will be reported by Moen in chapter 4.

No model or theory should remain unchallenged. Each challenge strengthens the theory, for it validates the original model and theory or specifies new conditions or raises new questions. Kirkendall's operational model which was used in California to test the explanatory model was used by LeDoux[8] to test the model in New Mexico. At that time and in that state more than half of the districts were moving downward in at least two of the operational variables, while in the California study all districts were up in all variables. The result in New Mexico was a poorer predictive value for the model than previously demonstrated. This led LeDoux and Burlingame[9] to challenge the explanatory model originally presented by Iannaccone and Lutz.[10] LeDoux's study, its findings, and a reanalysis of those data are presented by Burlingame in chapter 5.

Based on the questions raised in the LeDoux-Burlingame article, Lutz[11] responded regarding the nature of the explanatory model, proposing some changes in the operational model and the addition of a new variable operationalizing the "gap" between the school board and the school district proposed in the original explanatory model, which was assumed but never measured by previous verification studies attempting to account for incumbent defeat. As a result of that response, Garberina[12] conducted a study of incumbent school board member defeat in Massachusetts. That study used the district's tax levy as an indicator of school board response to community change. This variable was assumed to be a measure of the gap between the board and the community identified in the explanatory model but not measured in prior verification studies. Gaberina's study was able to account for a large amount of the variance in "down" districts apparently left unaccountable in the LeDoux study.

Garberina presents these data and his findings in chapter 6. Based on his study, we are now attempting to *predict*, for the first time, the likelihood of school board incumbent defeat.

In chapter 7 Mitchell analyzes the measurement problems that exist in this line of research and makes some suggestions for solving them. He also discusses methodological issues present in the formulation of various theories attempting to account for conflict and participation in local school district politics. He concludes that the "dissatisfaction theory" present in this work is even stronger than the present research and statistical significance levels indicate.

Another Branch from the Same Tree

Another parallel line of research is underway at this time. Based on the ethnographic description from which the original explanatory model was developed, a notion of school board council style was formulated. Explicit in the original field study was the fact that a school board develops a style of policy-making behavior over time. This behavior is governed by a set of norms that sanction the behavior of board members as well as that of certain central office staff. These norms are enhanced by a broader set of behaviors at the county, state, and national levels. Such behaviors are exhibited in various levels of school board association meetings and literature that operate as a socialization process to shape the values and behaviors of individual local boards and their members. Lutz identified this phenomenon as the "culture of school boards."[13] Later he posited a relationship between the council-like behavior of a local school board,[14] operationalized within the elite-arena continuum suggested by Bailey,[15] and the diversity of the community as measured by Lieberson.[16]

Using the elite-arena model, Gresson[17] studied two school boards, one identified as more elite, the other as more nearly arena. As a result of that ethnographic description of the two boards, the elite-arena model was modified, as related to school boards, to include mock elite and mock arena behavior of school boards. That study lead to the identification of the anomic behavior of school boards in conflict, which appears to have considerable meaning for school boards, incumbent defeat, and involuntary superintendent turnover. Following the same theoretical formulation but using a statistical design, Witmer[18] gathered data from a sample of 30 school districts in Pennsylvania in order to determine the relationships between council type, community diversity, and public satisfaction with the board and education. These data and their meaning for school board members and superintendents are reported in chapters 8 and 9.

Chapter 10 summarizes the dissatisfaction theory of democratic participation in local school policies and decision making. It recommends specific action for altering the culture of school boards and a revised type of school board response to community demands and conflict. Explicit suggestions are made to school board members who would like to be reelected and superintendents who might choose to keep their jobs following incumbent defeat. The dissatisfaction theory of local school politics is compared with Minar's conflict theory and Mann's administration representation theory. Suggestions for future research are included.

Summary

The original model identified certain conditions that resulted in a gap between the community and the school board. This gap often resulted in incumbent school board member defeat, followed by increased nonunanimous voting on the board, and within 3 years involuntary superintendent turnover. These notions were tested in the series of statistically designed verification studies previously mentioned.

As the results of these verification studies were available, we returned to the original model to ask what we now knew or what else needed to be known. This process required a return to some additional ethnographic work. Presently a study is underway that consists of a 12-month participant/observer study of an anomic school board. From this new branch of grounded research some other things may be hypothesized. It may be that our original variables in incumbent defeat and superintendent turnover represent the identification of symptomatic behaviors and not "causal" conditions.

The gap between the board and the community may well be the causal factor, and this may be identified best by the conflict resulting from the "gap" between the board's council-type behavior and the community's diversity. The original 19 socioeconomic-political variables may be only symptomatic of anomic board behavior. It may be that this cancer (anomic behavior) is caused by the virus of "the gap" and that the final result is "death" (involuntary superintendent turnover).

In addition to setting the stage for the reports of research in the following chapters, this preface has described a process of research that has resulted in both meaningful theory and practical answers. This process involves (1) careful ethnographic descriptions of important educational problems; (2) the development of explanatory models based on the ethnographic studies; (3) the formulation of testable hypotheses based on the grounded explanatory model; (4) conducting verification studies to test the hypotheses; (5) returning after each verification study to the model to ask how the model must be reformed; (6) returning when necessary to the description of the empirical world to explain new or divergent findings, thus developing new hypotheses; and finally (7) formulating a set of laws governing the phenomena in order to formulate a theory. Such a process has proved useful in the research outlined here and reported below.

Notes

1. Laurence Iannaccone and Frank W. Lutz, *Politics, Power and Policy: The Governing of Local School Districts* (Columbus, Ohio: Charles E. Merrill Publishing Co., 1970).

2. Peter Caws, "Operational, Representational and Explanatory Models," *American Anthropologists* (March, 1974).

3. Barney G. Glaser and Anselem Strauss, *The Discovery of Grounded Theory* (Chicago: Aldine Press, 1967).

4. Richard S. Kirkendall, "Discriminating Social, Economic and Political Characteristics of Changing versus Stable Policy-Making Systems in School Districts," unpublished Ph.D. dissertation, Claremont Graduate School, Claremont, California, 1966.

5. John C. Walden, "School Board Changes in Involuntary Superintendent Turnover," unpublished Ph.D. dissertation, Claremont Graduate School, Claremont, California, 1966.

6. Robert M. Freeborn, "School Board Changes on the Succession Pattern of Superintendents," unpublished Ph.D. dissertation, Claremont Graduate School, Claremont, California, 1966.

7. Allen W. Moen, "Superintendent Turnover as Predicted by School Board Incumbent Defeat in Pennsylvania's Partisan Elections," unpublished Ph.D. dissertation, The Pennsylvania State University, University Park, Pennsylvania, 1971.

8. Eugene P. LeDoux, "Outmigration: Its Relation to Social, Political and Economic Conditions and to the Governing of Local School Districts in New Mexico," unpublished Ph.D. dissertation, The University of New Mexico, Albuquerque, New Mexico, 1971.

9. Eugene P. LeDoux and Martin Burlingame, "The Iannaccone-Lutz Model of School Board Change: A Replication in New Mexico," *Educational Administration Quarterly* (Autumn 1973).

10. Iannaccone and Lutz, *Politics, Power and Policy*.

11. Frank W. Lutz, "The Role of Explanatory Models in Theory Building: In Response to LeDoux-Burlingame," *Educational Administration Quarterly* (Winter 1975).

12. William L. Garberina Sr., "Public Demand, School Board Response and Incumbent Defeat: An Examination of the Governance of Local School Districts in Massachusetts," unpublished Ph.D. dissertation, The Pennsylvania State University, University Park, Pennsylvania, 1975.

13. Frank W. Lutz, "School Baords as Socio-Cultural Systems" in Peter J. Cistone (ed.), *Understanding School Boards* (Lexington, Mass.: D.C. Heath, 1975), pp. 63-77.

14. Frank W. Lutz, "Cultures and Councils in Educational Governance," presented at the American Anthropological Association (San Francisco, 1975).

15. F.G. Bailey, "Decisions by Consensus in Councils and Committee" in Michael Banton (ed.), *Political Systems and the Distribution of Power* (London: Travistock Publications, 1965).

16. Stanley Lieberson, "Measuring Population Diversity," *American Sociological Review* (December 1969).

17. Aaron D. Gresson, III, "External-Internal Mandates and Elite-Arena Behavior in Local School Boards," unpublished Ph.D. dissertation, The Pennsylvania State University, University Park, Pennsylvania, 1976.

18. Daniel C. Witmer, "School Board Council Type—Community Diversity and Public Attitude about School," unpublished D.Ed. dissertation, The Pennsylvania State University, University Park, Pennsylvania, 1976.

**Public Participation in
Local School Districts**

1 Cultures and Conflict in Local School Districts

Margaret A. Ramsey

Introduction

One might question why a book on the politics of local school districts begins with a chapter of anthropology, culture, and conflict. The fact is that the study of education is best approached on an interdisciplinary basis. Thus, the dissatisfaction theory explicated in this book rests on various sociological, economic, and political factors related to conflict, and anthropological models offer some of the better attempts to integrate these concepts within a theory of culture.

This chapter will briefly develop the history of events in anthropology and education that have lead anthropologists to be interested in education and educationists to be interested in anthropological methods. Certain facets in the development of professionals in both anthropology and education are painted as having contributed to something less than a satisfactory state of knowledge and application as these two areas had attempted to merge into a subdiscipline of educational anthropology.

Finally, by relying heavily on Le Vine's[1] effort to bring the works of sociologists, economists, political scientists, and psychological-psychiatric theorists into a synthesized theory, a culture and conflict is explicated that parallels the variables utilized in the dissatisfaction theory of local school governance.

Problems in Studying Educational Cultures

Anthropologists have reached a curious spot in history. No longer exclusively "in Her Majesty's Service," anthropologists can be found in every nation of the world. Each nation seems well supplied with anthropologists, armed with the objectivity that participant observation furnishes them. Each national university lectures young neophytes on the serious dangers of the field research and "going native." Although nations, tribes, and organizational units may be studied ethnographically, their political beliefs may not be conducive to furthering open field research, understanding, and sometimes even economic development.

Although no longer in Her Majesty's Service, anthropologists hunger for grants-in-aid and travel funds and find, all too often, that their "pure research" has certain economic restrictions, governmental imperatives, developmental needs, and other such bugaboos. There are innoculations, language barriers, visas,

1

and other red tape to wade through, to say nothing of the age-old territorial imperative held by many groups, keeping the intruder/stranger too busy to really see what is happening or even keeping researchers out at all costs. For such reasons many present anthropologists decide to look elsewhere for field data.

As grants to study exotic cultures become more difficult to procure, many social-minded anthropologists began to express their concern for the state of their own country and culture. After all, many said, why go off to the exotic, when plenty of institutions need researching here at home? So at the dissertation stage, doctoral candidates were released from the difficult task of procuring funds for travel if a study could be tailored to a topic "at home." Obviously the Pacific/Oceania, Asian, or African major was out of luck.

For those who could label themselves as urban or educational anthropologists, the cities and schools of America offered virgin territory for ethnography. Since human beings suffer from the same syndromes of those they would study, most of these anthropologists were curiously ethnocentric, if not even a bit narrow-minded. Most of these "straight" anthropologists had limited actual experience in schools. The urban types produced some of the very worst in extremism in social viewpoints. Moynihan and Glazer's study[2] of poor minority groups reflects that type of report. When "educational anthropologists" did write of schools, it was generally of the school as a social system.

The "ethnography of the classroom" was another pitch, focused narrowly, too often ignoring the important "holistic" relationships that should be the hallmark of anthropological studies. Perhaps this focus on the individual school and classroom occurs so frequently not because of the development of anthropological research at the time, but because of the scope of the researcher's experience and the availability of access to a social system. Most researchers did not have, and still do not have, the credentials and/or experience to be your on-the-spot, native-superintendent, participant/observer. Most anthropological/ sociological participant observation was, and to some extent still is, done by people who become and/or were previously teachers.

As anthropology assumed greater importance in education, during the 1950s and 1960s more graduate students selected ethnographic methods as an alternative to statistical methods in their dissertations. Given their roles, the easiest source of field data for their dissertations was their daily classroom experience, a fairly novel idea at the time. Such practices help explain why the graduate student in educational anthropology tends, or did tend, to focus on the classroom. In such a way, entry, always a problem for the ethnographic researcher, was provided for classroom teacher participant/observer who chose to study the classroom. However, entry and data availability are not sufficient to explain the rather limited focus of the educational anthropologist.

Anthropologists who see the school as an alien culture will be most likely to limit their focus to the classroom and/or the school. Such researchers can be likened to some anthropologists who studied the potlatch of the Northwest

Coast Indians. By looking at the activity alone and neglecting the seasonal changes of weather, resource availability, network alliances, etc., many anthropologists failed to realize that the potlatch was a system, and not just an isolated and sporadic custom. They were correct as far as they had looked. By only seeing the first level, they failed to grasp the meaning and significance of the potlatch. In similar fashion, anthropologists often fail to see the school as part of a network, with variations within a larger pattern. The teacher and classroom are important, but the key in any social-cultural system is looking at its variables, patterns of systematic relationships, and the participants and the environmental network that supports the system.

Few anthropologists discuss the school as part of a school district. There are exceptions, most notably Wolcott.[3] The notion that a school board is a culture unto itself, though part of a general society, is one that is generally strange to them. For all the admonitions about cultural bias, most anthropologists cannot help, at this time, holding intellectually restrictive views of schools. They are limited by training, lack of interest and/or knowledge of the educational bureaucracy that exists, and general unwillingness to accept educators who "do" educational anthropology. This lack of acceptance is at least partially explained in the preceding description of the inadequacies often plaguing the educator-anthropologist.

If the anthropologist who decides to study schools and educational structures is an odd fellow, consider the plight of the educator-anthropologist. This person comes to use the tools of anthropology (models, theories, and methods) as a means of studying and processing problems of education. The anthropologist does not quite recognize such a creature or "know how to classify him/her." This person usually is first an educator by training and experience. Often this person "came through education" and was certified as a teacher, counselor, principal, or superintendent. They have a knowledgeable idea of how a school system operates.

Why do most of these people also fail to see, in operational terms, the classroom, the school district, or the school board as a holistic system? Why, as true participant/observers, do most of these individuals fail to see the forest for the trees? As participant/observers, they usually hold or have held membership in the educational society. They have far fewer entry and access problems than do traditional anthropologists. Yet, they most often fail to act as change agents when one would think that the educator-anthropologist would have the best working knowledge of a school system, of how and why it might change.

Perhaps they fail because they are "the natives." They are too ingrained with and immersed in the beliefs of their "culture" to be able to identify and utilize or change those beliefs. Also, the superintendent or principal is restrained by "studying" his/her own culture. In similar fashion, "ways of behavior" are as prescribed and codified for the school board member as they are for the village council in the South Pacific. Sacred myth and ritual exist in every realm of the educational system. Such problems are not limited to the neophyte teachers, but, in fact, probably increase as one moves up the scale of the educational hierarchy. As Harwood[4] states for another society, "Myths stand behind the social order as charters, and give to social institutions an aura of rightness. That is to say, myths codify and sanction a set of activities, a set which Malinowski terms an institution."

Neither the existence of nor the belief in myths—nor their systematic suppression within a society—should handicap the investigator. In fact, the knowledge and examination of that phenomenon in education cannot be overlooked without faulting the ethnography. The *National School Board Journal* may not be the *pièce de résistance* of academic pedagogy, but it is the voice of the school board members and, as such, does fairly accurately reflect their own world view. If one is to assess what a culture thinks and believes, and if one is to attempt to explain why and how it acts, there is no better source than the culture itself. Excellent secondary sources for the ethnography of educational systems are the publications, daily communiques, minutes of meetings of the various groups of teachers, principal, etc. Nothing is ever quite like the primary source of data—observation of, and informant data from, the members of the society itself. It was vogue for a while, and in some places still is, to ask students about curriculum policy, rules, etc. It is somewhat bizarre that in a system supposedly devoted to educating the young, it would be considered novel to involve students in the educational decision-making process. On the other hand, researchers often learn that the expressed tenets of culture are not always the operational ones. If one views and explores the culture of schools from the position of power and policy making, the word *student*—let alone their views—may rarely, if ever, come into play. *Educating the masses* is another such interesting term that received some attention in the 1960s, but appears to this author to be anachronistic.

The main point in the above is that, without examining the expressed structure (the one visible and accessible) against the deeper structure (which may be neither readily accessible nor viewable), there is very little hope for either the educator-anthropologist or the anthropologist of education to understand or comprehend the educational structure. Both types of researchers, unaware of their limitations, not only view each other as "odd" or exotic, but often fail to grasp the meaning of the realities as well as the myths of educational bureaucracies. It is dangerous to carry the view of the school board as "exotic" too far. It is equally dangerous to become so immersed in the educational club that one can barely perceive school systems, let alone the rest of the world, which also has cultures which provide for education in some way.

The Function of Role and Myth in Conflict

So far this chapter has been devoted to explaining how different researchers view education and the process that led them to their particular bias. An examination of the notion of the myth as it operates in the school system has also been discussed. It is extremely important to understand who is observing and perceiving; and some notions about why they see it in the way they do is almost as important as what they see. Context, therefore, must never be forgotten by the ethnographer, for it provides an essential focus for the research. Harwood speaks of "the axis of space and time" as possible demarcations between myths. All institutions need myths to survive. "Given that each mythical charter is tied to an institutional and that it is myth itself which serves [at least in part] to demarcate the boundaries between one institution and another, the puzzle arises as to the means by which the myths are kept separate so as to prevent the boundaries of the myths from blurring, and to keep myths from running together and coalescing."[5]

Just as what the observer (researcher) sees—and his/her myth absorption—is limited by his/her viewpoint or myth system, so is society's or the educational bureaucracy's view of the researcher similarly limited. Such ideological gaps often express themselves in myths involving stereotypes, such as "school board members are influential and hold property" or "school board members dislike collective bargaining." Ideological gaps account for much of the cultural conflict among the members of an educational system.

More prevalent and more difficult to ascertain is the nature of conflict, change, and deviance within the educational system. The educational system and the role of individuals, within groups and among groups, are perhaps best noted by the dissonance exhibited in perception, viewpoint, and mythical representation. Just as Raven, a creature of socio-religious invention among many native North American groups, represents a range of "meaning," from prankster to an all-consuming, destructive figure (exemplifying many conflicts found within that culture), the role of superintendent is viewed within a range of meaning from culture hero to fall-guy/flunky (a "source of all error"). The latter meaning is often expressed through the process of school board member incumbent defeat and superintendent turnover. Who views whom and the way that is explained serve as the focus of much of the politics of education.

Culture, Conflict and School Boards

Anthropologists often divide culture and conflict into more easily viewed institutions within the culture and the change and deviance exhibited within them. In essence, the old "we-they" idea is self-evident and not very useful in explaining how members within a culture view others and themselves and why. The ability to use contrasting general cultural models of conflict to understand and explain school boards and their operation rests on three basic premises: (1) there is a worldwide culture of education with some generally recognizable "universal" categories; (2) in the United States there is a national culture of education, depending upon and interacting with the larger socioeconomic-political structure, itself a recognizable facet and therefore representative of that larger culture; and, (3) the school board can be considered a unique culture. *Subculture* is probably a more correct term for a school board except for the fact that, like the cells of a body, though dependent on the entire and larger physical body, all subsystems of one type act as a complete unit and have a recognizable type, function, and characteristic behavior so that they can be referred to as an entity. It facilitates examinations of school boards to call them a culture.

Gluckman states the criteria for transferring paradigms are that they (1) duplicate the defined type, (2) can be applied to societies of different types, and (3) express a hypothesis which can be tested on a new range of facts. Thus, Gluckman finds one can test the kingship/rebellion model in the Zulu/Shaka assassination syndrome with equally predictable results because his original principles were logically consistent. Contrasted with other sets of principles, such as cross validation in field methods, logical deductions can be made from these relations to give others another method; logical deductions can be made against observable facts.[6]

Therefore, how many cultures handle conflict should serve as an available set of models on how school boards handle conflict and, more importantly, how the larger educational system and society handle conflict in the educational system and how the society "handles" school boards that reach a functionally disruptive point.

Culture may be seen as a kind of cognitive map by which individuals and groups interpret their world and which enables them to act purposely within it. Culture should not be thought of as behavior itself but rather the rules that underly and provide the basis for behavior.[7] Culture is the structural underpinning of society. Because of its immense importance to human society, whom it serves and yet is invented for and by, it is easy to see how anthropologist Leslie White[8] saw culture as superorganic. Carried to the extreme, however, the notion of culture as a superorganic determinant of behavior is dangerous. As Harris indicates, ". . . if culture determines how we behave, then what difference is there between a democratic and totalitarian regime other than the illusion to which the actors in the democratic milieu have been enculturated that they are "freer" to choose their individual and collective destinies?"[9]

Nature versus nurture is a frequent argument heard in educational circles. Does the culture, the school, the family, the church, the group determine the life of an individual? Are people force-fed the patterns of their lives, "from sex to art"?[10] Such questions are central to a view of culture. How each person views culture and his/her "place" within it, largely determines his/her actions within it, as well as reactions to it. Culture, conflict, change, and deviances are integrally related to how groups perceive their position in the larger society. Myths, whether of a religious or social-political nature, serve to reinforce and "shape" perceptions. Neither the individual nor groups have to call culture by its name to recognize its pervasive presence. Whether a group calls a counter-force "they," "the government," "the church," "our society," "folks," or "taxpayers," they are referring to culture, or aspects of it, or perhaps members of such groups within that culture. The deterministic view of culture as superorganic is less useful than it is one-sided. It ignores the general systems approach that more closely resembles the workings of nature as we know it. People "make" culture and interact within the rules and structure of the culture they "made."

School boards often tend to operate in a parochial or provincial fashion because of their perception of their own position within their culture. Some of that behavior is reinforced by the national mythology of educational politics and some by local perceptions and beliefs. Some of the perceptions people have built about school boards serves to promote a false sense of the importance and sanctity of such boards. Perhaps the easiest stereotype to identify is a notion that members of school boards are older, wealthier, more stable, and thus wiser than the average taxpayer. Whether or not that is true, school board members and others often act as if indeed it is reality; so myth becomes fact. School board members thus assume the sagelike quality of a council of elders, whether in fact they are sagacious or not, because our culture reinforces notions that wisdom equals age and wealth, especially when coupled with power. Why aren't people in homes for the aged particularly revered? Why aren't unemployed men and women of 50 years of age or above recruited for their sagacity as they are in some other cultures? The answer is that they lack power in our culture! So we discover that as with many of our predetermined cultural notions, there is usually a "Catch 22." A subculture within the larger culture can invent a culture for itself that, in time, is nonresponsive and no longer tolerated by its larger culture. School boards often act in such a fashion, becoming masters of the "if and the but." Should they invent too many such excuses and not respond sufficiently to the demands of their constituents, they will lose power, and individual members may lose their seats on the board. In discussing this tendency, it is necessary to understand the ways a culture views itself and how these views are elaborated within a framework of conflict, change, and deviance.

A Model for Understanding and Studying Culture and Conflict

As indicated earlier in this chapter, Le Vine[11] discusses a wide range of theoretical formulation accounting for deviance, conflict, and change in a cultural context. In his discussion he rates the proposed dichotomy between hard and soft institutions. The former type constrains and limits behavior, and the latter provides an arena where the individuals may express their own needs, resulting in the formation of such areas as ecology, settlement patterns, and social stratification within a society. Soft institutions, on the other hand, are "expressive" institutions which permit the expressive or affective aspects of individuals within the society including religion, magical belief, art, folklore, and the like.[12] He further notes that, following the bureaucratic formulations, Weber and Whitting[13] suggest a third class of value institutions serving to defend beliefs, thus reducing dissonance resulting from discrepancies between "motivational goals" and "reality demands." Such a formulation appears useful to the explanation of most political systems. However, as Le Vine notes, the dichotomy or trichotomy of institutions within a society, though "ingenious and plausible," is an "oversimplification" and recognized as such even by its proponents.

Economic Indicators

One of the three major groups of indicators in the dissatisfaction theory is economic. Le Vine notes that McClelland[14] has treated the economy as a projective rather than a maintenance system. Thus economic growth follows and results from individual economic entrepreneurial activity which, in turn, affects the occurrence in the society of individuals with high-need achievement motivations. Thus while clearly the economy affects and sets limits to choices of individuals within a society, just as surely choices, and values, of individuals affect the economy and the culture and society.[15] Therefore economics cannot be ignored in models of school board behavior. Each school board is an aggregate of individuals who act as one. If schools are becoming more like big business in terms of fiscal budgets and responsibilities, then, following McClelland, they quite clearly provide a projection of the economic indicators of the institution locally as well as suggesting direction within the overall national picture.

Political Indicators

Following the same line of reasoning, Le Vine[16] cites the work of Lasswell[17] in political institutions and Levinson[18] in bureaucratic institutions, stating that, "Political and bureaucratic roles do not simply prescribe behavior but also provide a public vehicle for the satisfaction of private motives."[19] In similar fashion, notes Le Vine, Spiro[20] has shown that political and economic roles not only shape the choices of people but respond to and provide for the fulfillment of inner needs as well as "societal demands."

Individual behavior related to the governance processes of local school boards may be usefully classified along a pressure-response continuum. One must recognize, however, according to Le Vine, that when collective activities (such as school board policy making) become institutionalized, these behaviors cannot be "responsive to or reflective of" the motives or desires of individuals in *simple* ways. Such institutionalized collective behavior is always a result of forces exerted by societal norms that limits the acceptable behaviors and the available alternatives for the fulfilling of personal needs and aspirations of the individual. Therefore, there is little margin for the consideration by school personnel, from school boards to school teachers, as members of the institutionalized bureaucracy, of specific demands of individuals in order to meet particular and personalized needs. Such a confrontation, therefore, often results in disagreement, frustration, and hostility.

The roles of school board members are probably even more vulnerable in terms of public censure than are those of teachers or principals with tenure. While teachers and principals are paid with tax dollars, the public is never so easily aroused as when the school board raises taxes through a millage increase while failing to respond to the public's specific and individual demands. Such godlike powers tend to stimulate high interest and concern in the general populace. The school board usually cites current raises in teacher salaries as the cause of the increase. Such measures and countermeasures place the educational constituencies of the cultural system at odds with one another.

Other Classificatory Variables

Returning again to oversimplified classification systems for attempting to explain conflict and change in cultural systems, Le Vine indicates that the nominal classification of institutions as either maintenance or projective systems is misleading. He suggests it is more useful to understand all institutions as "environments" that provide not only limits to the range of any alternatives available but also a multiple set of options. Thus institutions or environments specify parameters but do not dictate specific choices among available behaviors. Rather the actual pattern of individual behavior is a function of the individual's personality and needs, interacting with and limited by the degree to which his/her values are shared by others in the same social-cultural-institutional environment. As discrepancies occur, they may be viewed as opportunities for and pressure to bring about institutional change. Thus, observed behavior and belief, transmitted through myth, folklore, and social norms, are equally important in understanding culture, conflict, and change.

The society's concept of what constitutes an institution will have previously set limits for understanding conflict within the institution. However, the notion that behavior is either conforming or deviant according to an invariant set of "normative perceptions and proscriptions" with reward and punishment doled out according to conformity or the lack of it, does not account for a great deal of social behavior. Institutions are like "the tips of icebergs," says Le Vine. Most of what goes on is never visible to the public. Educators are fairly knowledgeable about that fact. Many believe that the higher the power or authority, the less one sees of the actual decision-making process. Even at "open" public board meetings, much of what is decided or voted upon has already been discussed and consensus was reached before the meeting. School superintendents call "briefing" meetings where often decisions are made prior to the announced meetings. Here decisions are made by the board and the superintendent's "chosed few." Conflict results when the gap between public expectations and school board behavior widens too far for any myth or explanation to explain it.

Actually behavior is not simply conforming or deviant, Le Vine points out, but is best classified along a continuous scale. Individual choices and everyday behaviors can be better recognized along such a continuum. The greater the number of checkpoints along the continuum on which one can specify behavioral differences and normative sanctions, the better. Le Vine suggests seven such positions or checkpoints: (1) behaviors that are forbidden and for which punishments are proscribed, but still the behaviors are not effectively eliminated within the society; (2) behaviors forbidden but which are not consistently punished or even universally regarded as punishable (i.e., activities illegal or socially forbidden under certain conditions but which are permitted when they are exhibited in nonpublic or restricted ways or magnitudes); (3) behaviors not prohibited or required, but which fall within an optional range of individual choice and come as somewhat of a surprise to others; (4) behaviors unconsciously expected by others, under certain conditions, but not specifically required (deviance is only recognized because of their absence—a deviance of commission by omission); (5) behaviors consciously expected but not specifically required, where convention requires the behavior but nevertheless the behavior is optional; (6) behavior required according to informal social norms and sanctioned within the informal system only; and (7) behaviors required by formal prescription and enforced by formal procedures such as explusion from the role position or other legal penalties. Within such a classification system, a specific behavior is not simply either conforming or deviant but varies in degree of conformity or deviance. Such categories are not usually discrete or mutually exclusive. The insistence of discrete categories in such cases only serves to "cloud the researcher's mind" as well as the public's view of individual and group behavior, such as that of school boards.[21] Conflict can often occur because one supposes decisions are made by "virtu sola" as opposed to "in context." The latter in-context notion of decisions and behaviors provides a much more useful and anthropological view of school board decision making.

Le Vine further suggests that deviance occurs in at least three ways: (1) as an exaggeration of norms, for example, when the superintendent insists on creating all policy for the board and the board allows it without question or opposition; (2) as a breakdown of norms, as when one or two board members refuse to join the majority on an issue, forcing a split vote in a public meeting; and (3) as a breakdown of norms, when the board is forced to debate issues totally and publically, voicing openly the public criticism usually kept below the "tip of the iceberg." This latter stage of deviance from school board norms is referred to in chapters 8 and 9 as anomic school board behavior.

Conflict, at some level, is a necessary catalyst for change, and change is a required feature of any adaptive group. A group must be able to adapt, or else it risks extinction. Humans survived and evolved, socially and genetically in groups, adaptation being necessary to survival. Groups, institutions, and cultures require social adaptation through resolution of conflict and change. Le Vine suggests four basic models of change: (1) persistence, (2) breakdown, (3) progress, and (4) revitalization.

Persistence describes the ability of a sociocultural system to meet and survive in changed macrosocial environments without drastically altering itself. *Breakdown* involves the disintegration of the old social order, resulting in a normlessness which can lead to a "psychopathology" caused by the stress of having to make new decisions and break with old traditions. The *progress* model requires that individuals in the culture either have skills needed to adapt to new activities required by the changed environment and the predisposition to do so or have a predisposition to change and be able to learn the new required behaviors through participation in the changing culture. Finally, the *revitalization* model incorporates elements of the former three models. Internal or external changes force a disruption of the culture's social equilibrium. This results in stress, disillusionment, and anxiety. Disruptive, normless behavior results. A new leader then emerges who is able to articulate a new "code" or value, a "synthesis of ideas drawn from the traditional ideological resources of the culture, ... but in any case is sharply contrasted with the existing but unsatisfying value system."[22] While this may sound like a rambling from Castaneda's *Journey to Ixtlan*[23] or an accurate description from the messianic movement in literature, it also (amazingly) resembles school boards, the personal rise to power, and group power struggles. Every incumbent speaks of stability, control, and/or discipline, as the situation demands. Every insurgent speaks of conflict and change. It seems that cultures maintain themselves through two basic adaptive processes: stability and change. Each episode of the stability— change process has a consequent set of behaviors that are periodically used to carry out the process.

Apparently either conformity to norms in social equilibrium or some type of normative adaption to the forces of environmental change is required in order for social systems to survive. The three major types of psychosocial adaptations, or bases for conformity to cultural norms, says Le Vine, are (1) willing conformity, (2) coerced conformity with motivational displacements, and (3) normative pluralism.[24] The behaviors for change are either institutionally induced or personality-induced. Those which are institutionally induced are changes in the context of normative demands for role performance or in the enforcement of such demands, changes in the opportunity structure, and changes in the scope and complexity of selective environments. Personality-induced changes include cultural drift, organizational competition and selection, and successful innovation within the existing opportunity structure.[25] Le Vine's model of cultural change can be successfully transferred to any cultural subgroup, school boards included. Models of school board behavior, such as the Iannoccone-Lutz dissatisfaction theory of local school governance proposed in this book, can be usefully viewed in this context.

Summary

This chapter has emphasized overall models of social theories on cultural conflict, change, and deviance. The fact that school boards fit many of the propositions should serve to reinforce the transferability of ideas and models and demonstrate that school boards can be studied and examined within generalized models of culture.

Notes

1. Robert A. Le Vine, *Culture, Behavior, and Personality* (Chicago: Aldine Publishing Company, 1973).

2. Daniel P. Moynihan and Nathan Glazer, *Beyond the Melting Pot* (Cambridge, Mass.: M.I.T. Press, 1963).

3. Harry F. Wolcott, *The Man in the Principal's Office* (New York: Holt, Rinehart and Winston, Inc., 1973).

4. Frances Harwood, "Myths, Memory, and the Oral Tradition: Cicero in the Trabrianes," *American Anthropologist,* vol. 78, no. 4 (December 1976), p. 785.

5. Ibid., pp. 785-6.

6. Max Gluckman, "The Difficulties, Achievements, and Limitations of Social Anthropology," in Robert A. Manners and David Kaplan (eds.), *Theory in Anthropology* (Chicago: Aldine Publishing Company, 1968), p. 42.

7. James P. Spradley and David M. McCurdy, (eds.), *Conformity and Conflict: Readings in Cultural Anthropology* (Boston: Little, Brown and Company, 1974), p. 2.

8. Leslie A. White, "Individuality and Individualism: A Cultural Interpretation," *Texas Quarterly* (1963) vol. 6, pp. 111-27.

9. Marvin Harris, *The Rise of Anthropological Theory* (New York: Columbia Press, 1968), p. 298.

10. Ibid.

11. Le Vine, *Culture, Behavior, and Personality,* pp. 85-98.

12. Ibid., p. 86.

13. John W.M. Whitting et al., "The Learning of Values" in E. Vogt and E. Albert (eds.), *The People of Remrock* (Cambridge, Mass.: Harvard University Press, 1966).

14. David C. McClelland et al., *The Achieving Society* (Princeton, N.J.: Van Nostrand Press, 1961).

15. Le Vine, *Culture, Behavior, and Personality,* p. 87.

16. Ibid.

17. Harold Lasswell, *Psychopathology of Politics* (Chicago: University of Chicago Press, 1930).

18. Daniel J. Levinson, "Role, Personality and Social Structure in the Organizational Setting," *Journal of Abnormal and Social Psychology,* vol. 58, pp. 170-80.

19. Le Vine, *Culture, Behavior, and Personality,* p. 87.

20. Melford E. Spiro, "Social Systems, Personality and Functional Analysis" in B. Kaplan (ed.), *Studying Personality Cross-Culturally* (Evanston, Ill.: Row, Peterson, 1961).

21. Le Vine, *Culture, Behavior, and Personality,* p. 89.

22. Ibid., p. 94.

23. Carlos Castaneda, *Journey to Ixtlan* (New York: Simon and Schuster, 1974).

24. Le Vine, *Culture, Behavior, and Personality,* pp. 138-4.

25. Ibid., pp. 153-5.

2 A Culture-Conflict Model of School Board Member Incumbent Defeat and Superintendent Turnover

As demonstrated in the previous chapter, the phenomena of school board member defeat and superintendent turnover can be usefully understood within a cultural model. In their original formulation of a model, describing and explaining school board member incumbent defeat and superintendent turnover, Iannaccone and Lutz[1] presented a model based largely on sociological notions.

The previous chapter suggests a general cultural model of that same political process. The advantage of the cultural model over the sociological one is perhaps obscured by the fuzzy and ill-defined line between sociology and anthropology. One way we conceive the difference between the cultural model presented here and the original sociological model is to say that the present model couches the discussion of the incumbent defeat-superintendent turnover phenomena in terms of the society and its culture and subcultures. This permits comparisons and conclusions to be made about this political phenomenon which have implications for the notion of cultural pluralism in education. Thus, one is able to suggest relationships between the politics of education and such empirically grounded educational programs as bilingual programs and school integration and bussing.

In his book *The Interpretation of Culture*, Geertz[2] states:

Undirected by culture patterns—organized systems of significant symbols—man's behavior would be virtually ungovernable, a mere chaos of pointless acts and exploding emotions, his experience virtually shapeless. Culture, the accumulated totality of such patterns, is not just an ornament of human existence but—the principal bases of its specificity—an essential condition for it. . . . Most bluntly [this] suggests that there is no such thing as a human nature independent of culture. . . . Without men, no culture, certainly; but equally, and more significantly, without culture, no men. . . .

Thus, it seems imperative to place important political processes in a cultural context if "man's behavior is virtually *ungovernable*" without it. Further, it seems clear that the original model implicitly saw the school district as a culture with values, beliefs, needs, wants, etc., and the local school board as a subculture (since culture is defined by Geertz as ". . . a set of central mechanisms—plans, recipes, rules, instructions . . . —for the governing of behaviors").[3]

Iannaccone and Lutz envisioned that not only might the school district and the school board be separate (or relatively separate) systems, but also, as separate cultural systems, they could reach a state where they were *different*

15

enough to produce not only conflict but political revolution in its more sane form—incumbent defeat and administrative turnover. The model postulates that when the gap between what the larger culture believes to be governance "appropriate to the temper of its people" and the reality of that governance becomes sufficiently great, then the people will act so as to modify that government through the elective process, resulting in incumbent school board member defeat and usually followed by superintendent turnover.

If one accepts the proposition that many school districts, certainly large metropolitan-type districts, encompass a degree of internal diversity often seen as "cultural hodgepodge," one may ask some questions about the school district (its diverse culture) and the correspondence of the governance system (the school board's policy process) to that diverse culture. Here we paraphrase questions asked by Geertz[4] of exotic cultural systems:

1. Can all groups safely and effectively contend within the governance system provided? or Has all but one group effectively been eliminated from the process?
2. Is the governance process enacted by the school board appropriate to the temper of the people?
3. Has the school board refused and/or failed to come to terms with the fact of internal diversity within the school district?
4. Given the answers to the above, what can one predict about incumbent school board member defeat and involuntary superintendent turnover?

This model was intended to provide answers to these questions. But, for the model, the answers are relatively unimportant. The important thing is the question. Are we asking the right questions? When we get the answers, will we be able to make suggestions for the improvement of the governance of local public education as well as make some predictions about what will occur if such changes are effected? In the belief that these questions, couched in the concept of culture, provide better questions and therefore lead to more meaningful answers, the following is undertaken.

The School District and Cultural Pluralism

As a major concept in the model, cultural pluralism, as contrasted with structural pluralism, is important to understand. Sanday[5] has neatly contrasted the two, with particular reference to education. In her book *Anthropology and the Public Interest,* Sanday notes that for the most part structural pluralism has existed and operated through the governance process in public education to the advantage of some groups, comprised largely of upper- and middle-class people, and to the disadvantage of others, comprised largely of minority and lower-class people. Writing with Jacob, she notes: "More frequently than not, the outcome [of the cultural differences within a school district] is one in which differences are exacerbated rather than reduced, with the result that the minority group member is often excluded from further meaningful interaction."[6] For the minority public school student, she notes that this means "dropped out." For the citizen in general it means in Geertz's terms effectively eliminating all groups but one from the governance process. Such a result is best defined as *structural pluralism,* a condition in which cultural differences result in the formulation and maintenance of a class or caste system that is relatively inflexible and that relegates culturally different groups to widely different positions, opportunities, and reward systems within the society. On the other hand, *cultural pluralism* is ". . . conceptualized in terms of variation in contemporary cultural themes, information components, and behavior styles within and across ethnically defined groups. . . , education and public policy must take these differences into consideration."[7] Thus, cultural pluralism provides different alternatives and routes toward equal participation consistent with cultural differences. In such a way, cultural pluralism provides variations and alternatives for different cultural groups in order to participate, accomplish, and achieve; whereas structural pluralism relegates different cultural groups to their "proper" states of participation, accomplishment, and achievement, resulting in the type of class system still all too operative in our nation and the world.

Cultural Homogeneity Versus Heterogeneity

The above discussion is based on the notion that a society may possess a culture that varies from homogeneous to heterogeneous. "Cultural homogeneity implies that there is one scale along which life styles exhibited by members of a given society can be judged and understood."[8] In the United States, the "melting pot" theory of culture, based on an Anglo-Saxon ethic, is such a culture. Heterogeneous cultures exist in societies which, while they may have a "mainstream" culture, allow, encourage, and cherish separate subcultures to flourish within and parallel to that "mainstream." In such societies individuals may be classified, according to Sanday, as:

1. *Mainstream*: functionally assimilated into the culture that dominates and operates the society.
2. *Bicultural*: can operate effectively in both the mainstream culture and another cultural unit.
3. *Culturally different*: functionally assimilated into a cultural unit different from the mainstream culture.
4. *Culturally marginal*: less than functionally assimilated into any cultural unit, i.e., peer group that has disassociated itself from a foreign-born parent's culture but failed as yet to become mainstream.[9]

In a heterogeneous culture there are parallel scales along which any set of behaviors may be judged. If the culture is structurally pluralistic, values or ranks are assigned to each scale, usually with "mainstream" being assigned the highest status and "culturally marginal" the lowest. In such a society, the society and their schools assign to members from these different cultural groups separate statuses, in descending order, each depreciating the values, norms, customs, needs, and aspirations of the next lower cultural rank. These ranks carry privilege and opportunity in different measure to the disadvantage of the successively lower cultural type.

When the heterogeneous culture is culturally pluralistic, the society provides alternative sets of activities and opportunities enabling equal participation and achievement within the society, regardless of cultural type. One is not assigned a status as a result of cultural type; one is able to choose a route of participation in the larger society that seems to that individual most appropriate based on his or her own cultural situation.

To provide some cultural group or type other than mainstream with special privilege equal to or even above that afforded to the mainstream culture does not make the society culturally pluralistic, but is merely neostructural pluralism, which puts individuals from other culture units at a disadvantage and still assigns them to lower rank in the class society that still exists. In order to obtain a culturally pluralistic society, the fundamental requirement is for the society to structure within itself different alternative opportunities so that it is possible for all persons, regardless of cultural group or type, to participate and achieve based on only the individual's capacity and not upon the status assigned to his/her cultural unit or type.

In *The Passage of Power,* Burling notes: "A major contribution of western civilization has been the development of the democratic process of participation in the governance of people."[10] He further points out that in the United States this process has come to fruition mainly within the structure of mass political parties, providing an arena for reducing ". . . the gap between the government and the people, between legislative factions and the popular interests. . . ." He then says, "Where heredity is gone and republican [representative] government has not taken place, we must ask what has arisen instead." If, as is the case, public education has largely rejected the politics of parties as an alternative means to inherited power in the governance of local education, "we must ask what has arisen instead."

Lutz[11] has demonstrated that local school boards, governing public education, have developed a political culture, rejecting the politics of political parties and replacing it with a type of structural pluralism, composed of individuals from the mainstream culture (largely WASP politics), that tends to advantage persons within the mainstream culture and disadvantage those of other cultural types. Equating the normal "sacred politics of education"[12] with elite councils as opposed to the alternative arena council, based on Bailey,[13]

Lutz proposes a relationship between the nature of the culture (homogeneous-heterogeneous) and the council type of the local board (elite-arena). Specifically he hypothesizes that the more heterogeneous the culture of the school district, the more arena (representative of factions or subcultures in the district) the local board should be. Lutz suggests that when many subcultures exist within the school district community and when the local school board acts in an elite council fashion (representative of the WASP class structure) and as trustees for, rather than representatives of, the diverse culture, dissatisfaction and conflict will be generated within the community.

Minar[14] suggested that the separation of education from the usual political style may generate conflict and opposition to education governance in local schools. "Whereas, in most democratic governments, structured conflict is recognized as the way the game is played, in school government it often seems to be regarded as a rude and foreign intrusion."[15] Based on his empirical findings, Minar indicates that such conflict is often correlated with lower-class school district composition while middle- and upper-class school districts generate less conflict in school governance. Perhaps this is because school boards, governing in a fashion dictated by the "culture of school boards," tend to advantage persons holding upper- and middle-class cultural values and disadvantage persons of lower-class cultural values. School boards tend to be comprised of mainstreamers, and other cultural types tend to be excluded from participation, in typical fashion of a structural pluralistic society. As the gap between the ruling group and the nonmainstreamers becomes sufficiently wide and those who are neither mainstreamers nor bicultural become sufficiently powerful, conflict escalates and results in the incumbent defeat of school board members and eventually in superintendent turnover.

A Model of Culture, Conflict, and Local School District Governance

The above discussion suggests the following model of the relationships between culture, conflict, and governance. Figure 2-1 explains conflict where culture is homogeneous within the society (or school district). Figure 2-2 explains conflict where culture is heterogeneous or diverse within the society or school district. Conflict is described in these figures from low conflict to high conflict on a nominal scale from 1 (low) to 5 (high).

Figure 2-1 predicts that when there is little cultural diversity within a school district and the nature of the society is best described as structural pluralism, elite council behavior is a good fit generating very little conflict and almost no incumbent defeat. The superintendent, operating as part of that council and within the norms of the culture of the school board, is not likely to be replaced because of the unlikely event of incumbent defeat. On the other hand, an arena

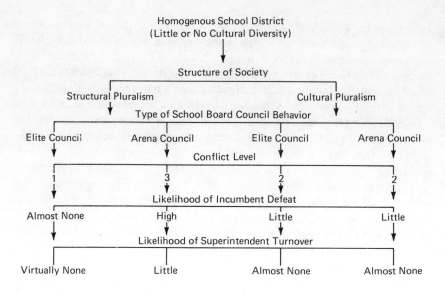

Figure 2-1. Model of Conflict in Homogeneous School Districts

council is not in phase with either the school district culture or the structure of the society (although this is not very likely to occur under these circumstances). It is likely to generate considerable conflict both within itself and between itself and the monolithic public. The likelihood of incumbent defeat is high; but the superintendent who has acted within the traditional segment of the board, in tune with the class-structured society and in the best interest of the mainstream, is relatively safe. The power shift is likely to be in the direction of bringing the board toward more elite behavior in support of the mainstream culture and the superintendent.

While a homogeneous culture might be structured according to a cultural pluralism, it is not likely; and if it existed, it would be difficult to recognize operationally. Having only mainstream individuals, such a society would structure itself and articulate norms that would allow alternative opportunities to other cultural types, if they existed. In such a case, the arena board would debate philosophical positions but be unable to represent culturally different groups, for they would not exist. Thus, a board with arena norms would behave only a little differently from a board with elite norms since there would be only one group to represent. In such a situation there is little likelihood of conflict, incumbent defeat, or superintendent turnover. It should be suggested that the superintendent whose behavior (trustee-delegate) conformed to the norms of the board type (elite-arena) would be least likely to lose his job.

A brief explanation of the above prediction regarding the superintendent is

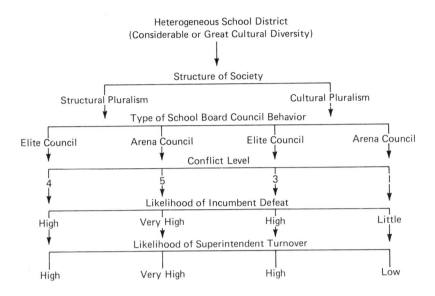

Figure 2-2. Model of Conflict in Heterogeneous School Districts

in order. Mann[16] has analyzed the behavior of administrators related to their dispositions regarding responsiveness to the public. At one end of the continuum is the administrator trustee who acts in the best interest of the public, as does the elite board. At the other end of the continuum is the "delegate" who acts as the public directs, in our case as directed by the majority vote of an arena school board representing a more or less diverse public. Thus, a trustee-type superintendent is more attuned with the elite board behavior and the traditional "culture of school boards," and a delegate-type superintendent is more attuned with an arena board and cultural pluralism. An alternative, the "politico" type administrator (one who selectively alternates between trustee and delegate), may also be recommended for most arena boards and less frequently for elite boards. As a "mixed behavior" it is more difficult to predict except as it tends more toward either the trustee or the delegate ends of the continuum.

In figure 2-2, heterogeneous school districts are analyzed. Such districts may be structurally pluralistic or culturally pluralistic. In the first case an elite board would be in tune with the existing structure of society and in conflict with the emerging subcultures which are looking for participation in and reward from that society. Since they tend to be "kept down" by the class structure of the society, since their values are not represented by the decisions that the board makes in elite fashion to the advantage of the mainstream, as this gap widens and membership in other subculture types increases, the conflict increases and the likelihood of incumbent defeat increases. A "trustee" superintendent, wed to the incumbent elite board, will likely suffer involuntary turnover following that incumbent defeat. His or her ability to survive such a defeat will likely depend on prior ability to exhibit "politico" behavior and move still further toward the "delegate" end of the continuum following the first incumbent defeat.

If the board acting for this heterogeneous-type district, exhibiting structural pluralism, governs in arena fashion, it is likely that their arena behavior is emerging and of recent vintage. In such a case they may well find themselves in conflict with their own norms governed by the traditional culture of school boards and akin to the structure of the traditional society. As noted in chapter 9, such a board finds itself "normless" and in a state of anomie. Such a condition may be predicted to be fraught with high conflict and even suicidal behavior. Incumbent defeat is very likely, and superintendent turnover most surely will follow. Again the politico-type superintendent is more likely to survive although even this type of administrator runs a high risk.

If the school district is culturally diffuse (heterogeneous) and the societal structure is culturally pluralistic, the elite council is likely to be a vestige of the past, having survived the transformation from structural pluralism to cultural pluralism with incumbent defeat. This is an unlikely occurrence; but if it exists (largely because of the "sacred" nature of educational politics), there will likely be rather high conflict, and incumbent defeat may be expected. Again the politico delegate type of superintendent is more likely to survive such an incumbent defeat. It is more likely that the superintendent in such a case also will be a vestige of the past and be a trustee-type administrator wed to the old elite board. Such a superintendent will probably not survive.

If in the above situation, however, the board behaves in arena fashion, it is congruent with the cultural pluralistic structure of that heterogeneous society, and little conflict is predicted. The likelihood of incumbent defeat depends solely on how well the arena board members represent in delegate fashion the nature of the culturally different society. It is most likely that incumbent defeat results from criminal or immoral acts of individual members. Involuntary superintendent turnover is unlikely when the administrative style is delegate (representing the wishes of the community as expressed by a majority vote of the arena board) and high as he attempts to operate in trustee fashion in opposition to the political nature of the arena board.

As noted above, Minar[17] in his article on school board conflict pointed to the correlation between conflict and the socioeconomic composition of the district and its board. It is likely that Minar was observing, on the one hand, an elite board in a structurally pluralistic society, within a homogeneous culture which, as predicted, generates little conflict. On the other hand, he likely observed either an elite or an arena council type of board in a relatively culturally heterogeneous school district, which resulted in rather high conflict.

The model suggested here may be a step toward a more conceptual model than one that relies solely on socioeconomic status (SES) as a predictor. The present model permits SES as a variable to be accounted for. But it also requires that the type of operational diversity within the culture and the composition of the board, as well as its governance style, be considered.

Summary

The model suggested here relies on three predictive conceptual variables: (1) the cultural diversity of the school district (from homogeneous to heterogeneous); (2) the structure of the society (from structural pluralism to cultural pluralism); (3) the nature of the school board's council behavior (from elite to arena). Based on the assessment of the school district's culture and the structure of its society, one can postulate a demand system. Based on the board's council behavior, its output can be specified. Given these assessments, one can determine whether a gap exists between the school district community and the school board that it claims to serve. As the distance between the board and the community (the gap) is wide, conflict will be high. As the distance between the two narrow, conflict will be low. Thus, the degree of political conflict likely within the school district is predictable. It is suggested that this conflict, caused by the gap described, results in meaningful predictions about school board member incumbent defeat and the likelihood of that political event's being followed by superintendent turnover.

In the chapters that follow the ability of certain socioeconomic-political indicators to operationalize these concepts and to account for the political phenomena of school board member incumbent defeat and superintendent turnover is described.

Notes

1. Laurence Iannaccone and Frank W. Lutz, *Politics, Power and Policy: Governing Local School Districts* (Columbus, Ohio: Charles E. Merrill, 1970).

2. Clifford Geertz, *The Interpretation of Culture* (New York: Basic Books, Inc., 1973).

3. Ibid., p. 44.

4. Ibid., p. 315.

5. Peggy Reeves Sanday (ed.), *Anthropology and the Public Interest* (New York: Academic Press, 1976).

6. Ibid., p. 95.

7. Ibid., pp. 60-61.

8. Ibid.

9. Ibid.

10. Robins Burling, *The Passage of Power* (New York: Academic Press, 1974).

11. Frank W. Lutz, "Local School Boards as Sociocultural Systems" in Peter J. Cistone (ed.), *Understanding School Boards* (Lexington, Mass.: Lexington Books, 1975).

12. See Iannaccone and Lutz, *Politics, Power and Policy.*

13. F.G. Bailey, "Decisions by Consensus in Councils and Committee" in Michael Banton (ed.), *Political Systems and the Distribution of Power* (London: Travistock Publications, 1975).

14. David Minar, "Community Politics and School Boards," *The American School Board Journal* (March 1967), pp. 33-37.

15. Ibid.

16. Dale Mann, *The Politics of Administrative Representation* (Lexington, Mass.: Lexington Books, 1976).

17. Minar, "Community Politics."

3

Antecedents to Incumbent Defeat and Superintendent Turnover

John Walden

The research reported in this chapter was conducted in southern California in the mid-1960s. The data collection period extended from 1951 through 1965, a period which seems almost remote when one considers the political turmoil which the nation has experienced since that time. In order to provide some perspective on the studies and the setting in which they were conducted, one must have some insight into the nature of suburban southern California communities during the two decades subsequent to World War II.

The Setting for the Studies

Four southern California counties and 117 of their school districts provided the setting for the research. The data collection period included a time when all the counties and their many school districts experienced rapid growths in population. It was the era of the G.I. tract home. Orange groves disappeared, replaced overnight, it seemed, with hundreds of houses straining unsuccessfully to look different from one another. Thousands seeking the "good life" left large cities such as Los Angeles and moved to the suburbs. In addition, large numbers of people packed their bags in the Midwest, East, and South and moved West, motivated to some degree by some of the same reasons which provided California with population booms in earlier periods of the state's history.

Local school districts throughout the four-county area studied suddenly found themselves without adequate facilities and staff to house and serve mushrooming school enrollments. Double sessions, even triple sessions, were not uncommon. Bond issues and tax referenda repeatedly were approved by voters anxious to provide classrooms for their children.

It was an era of population shifts as well as influxes. Many communities, which for years had had relatively stable and homogeneous populations, suddenly found themselves with strangers in their midst. The newcomers frequently differed from those who had lived most of their lives in these suburban cities and towns. Coming as they did not only from other parts of California, but also from throughout the nation, the recent arrivals often held different values and had different goals from the old-time residents and their leaders. School board members and superintendents, who for years had quietly directed the educational programs in their school districts, began to find their policies, even their formal positions of leadership, challenged by the newcomers. Such challenges, when they occurred, not only threatened political incumbents in the usual sense of the term, but also posed a similar problem for local superintendents.

Generally speaking, the setting for the studies was school districts which could be characterized as having enjoyed long periods of political stability, punctuated only occasionally with short periods of political unrest. Community populations were growing rapidly, values clashed, and periods of political stability were becoming shorter. Political strife, shaped not only by conditions within communities, but also by forces at the state and national levels, was increasingly common.

The Theoretical Framework

The studies focused on involuntary turnover in the superintendency as a consequence of the defeat for reelection of an incumbent school board member, the selection of a replacement for the outgoing chief school officer, and social and economic indicators which might be used to predict the defeat of incumbents for reelection to the board of education and the subsequent superintendent turnover.

The theoretical framework for the studies can be stated briefly.[1] First, it was assumed that changing socioeconomic conditions within a community would proceed to changes in the values, aspirations, and interests of that community. Second, it was assumed that a community's values, goals, and interests would be reflected in the community's decision-making structure, including the board of education. Third, it was assumed that changes in values, aspirations, and interests within a given community, as they were not reflected in more stable governing bodies, would tend to give rise to competition for control of the decision-making processes of the community, including the school board. The superintendent was conceptualized as heavily involved in the established local school district's policy-making process. It was assumed, therefore, that the chief school officer would come to be closely identified with the incumbent members of the board of education and that position would be vulnerable, should they suffer defeat. Perceived as an integral part of the policy-making system of the school district, the superintendency would be threatened by the control of that system passing into the hands of a new group.

Membership on boards of education changes frequently, not only at election time but between elections as well. An attempt was made to distinguish between conflict and nonconflict changes. It was assumed that vacancies which occurred on boards between elections and which were filled through appointment by the remaining board members would not constitute a shift in the political orientation of the board since it was likely that the appointing members would select for a colleague one who shared their values. Furthermore, it seemed logical to assume that changes in school board membership as a result of uncontested elections would not constitute a shift in the political orientation of the board. It was held that the "in" group would not voluntarily abandon its seats on policy-making bodies and that an emergent group would have to gain its seats by virtue of winning a contested election.[2]

The defeat of one or more incumbent school board members for reelection was considered evidence of rejection of the old policy-making system. Given the foregoing, one would expect to find significantly more turnover in the office of superintendent subsequent to school board elections in which incumbents were defeated than following elections in which no incumbents were unseated. Incumbent defeat also might be described as involuntary turnover on the school board. Therefore, if incumbent defeat signified rejection of the current policy-making system and if it was equally valid that the chief school officer was perceived as an integral member of that system, then it might be expected that involuntary turnover on the school board would often be followed by involuntary turnover in the office of superintendent.

The nature of turnover was the central focus of the study. The initial test was to determine the significance of superintendent turnover subsequent to a change in the composition of the board of education. All 117 school districts in four southern California counties which had five-member school boards and which had not undergone any boundary changes between 1956 and 1965 were selected for the study. In each district, school board members were elected by popular vote, and each superintendent was appointed to office by the board of education.

Data Collection and Findings

Data on all school board election and board membership changes as well as all changes in the superintendency were recorded. The initial analysis of the data on superintendent turnover and school board incumbent defeat left little doubt that a significant relationship existed between the two events. Significantly more turnover in the superintendency occurred after an incumbent school board member was defeated for reelection than occurred following the seating of school boards which had not undergone such a change. The relationship was significant at the .001 level.

A relationship was also demonstrated between the political instability of school districts and incumbent defeat. Following the procedure previously used by the Kammerer group in their study of the political role of the city manager,[3] superintendents who had assumed office following an incumbent board member's defeat were asked to render a judgment, by means of a questionnaire, on the stability of the politics of their school districts during their predecessor's tenure. Matching the responses of the superintendents to the question of political stability with the data regarding incumbent defeat gave an indication of the validity of using incumbent defeat as a reflection of the stability of school district politics. The respondents' responses were matched with the independently gathered election data, and the resultant contingency table clearly linked incumbent defeat to political instability in the school district. The significance was again at the .001 level.

The data strongly suggested that not only were defeat of incumbent school board members for reelection and political instability of school districts related, but also that incumbent defeat is a reflection of a struggle for power between an emergent power clique and an incumbent group. In short, analyses of these data provided an indication of the validity of the theoretical basis of the study; i.e., changes in the value orientations of a community will in turn lead to a challenge of the incumbent power structure by an emergent group. Incumbent defeat, then, is both a result of and an indicator of this conflict.

The next step was to determine the nature of superintendent turnover. Involuntary turnover was conceptualized as instances where the superintendent was asked to leave, was dismissed, was not offered a contract renewal, or left because of conflict with the school board. Voluntary turnover was characterized as cases where the chief school officer retired or left the school district either with evidence of support from the board or at least without evidence of conflict with the board.

Each case of superintendent turnover was classed as either voluntary or involuntary. Then these data were matched with the political stability of the school districts as described by the superintendent respondents (table 3-1). Involuntary turnover seemed clearly related to political instability. Significance was attained at the .001 level. It was of interest to note that in only a single instance did a respondent indicate voluntary turnover in the superintendency where political instability was indicated.

The second contingency table in this series matched voluntary-involuntary turnover with old school boards (boards in which no incumbents had been defeated) (table 3-2). Significance was attained at the .01 level.

Table 3-1
School District Political Stability and Superintendent Turnover

School District Political Stability	Voluntary Superintendent Turnover	Involuntary Turnover[a]
Stable	44	16
Unstable	1	27

Chi square = 36.18; $N = 87$

[a]One respondent did not reply to the question regarding political stability of the school district.

Table 3-2
Old and New School Boards and Superintendent Turnover

School Boards	Voluntary Superintendent Turnover	Involuntary Turnover[a]
Old	31	15
New	15	27

Chi square = 8.818; N = 88

[a]One respondent did not reply to the question regarding political stability of the school district.

Thus, it appeared clear that where school district politics were rather stable. With few controversial policy questions to cause division in the community, school board members suffered few defeats in their bids for reelection, and superintendent turnover, when it occurred, was likely to be voluntary. In contrast, where political instability was evident incumbent defeat frequently occurred, and the chief school officer's leaving was apt to be involuntary.

Two more tests of the voluntary-involuntary data were made. In these tests only those instances of superintendent turnover were used in which there appeared to be no possibility of error in judgment on the voluntary-involuntary question. There were 54 such cases. The resultant tables produced chi-square values which reached the .001 level of significance. There seemed to be little question, then, that incumbent defeat and involuntary turnover in the superintendency were significantly related.

Incumbent defeat did appear to signal the representation of an emergent power structure on the school board. There was evidence that incumbent defeat was linked to controversies over policy questions. This suggests that values were in conflict and that old values, aspirations, and political orientations were being challenged by new ones. In order for the new ones to be heard, thus having an effect upon the decision-making processes of the school district, it seemed necessary to successfully challenge the incumbent power structure *at the ballot box*.

Further, the data strongly suggested that the chief school officer was perceived as a policy maker and as a member of the incumbent decision-making structure. When the incumbent power group was challenged and defeated, the superintendent's position was vulnerable. More often than not, the superintendent departed.

A study parallel to the one just discussed looked at the succession patterns of superintendents in terms of the voluntary-involuntary turnover question.[4] It was hypothesized that when the chief school officer's departure from the school district was involuntary, then the successor would be an outsider. On the other hand, it was expected that candidates from the school district would stand a good chance of being selected as superintendent when the latter's departure was voluntary. The data confirmed the hypotheses, lending additional support to the theoretical basis for the studies. In this instance it was clear that a new power group represented on the school board desired as superintendent someone who was not identified with the old chief school officer and the establishment.

The final study to be discussed focused on social, economic, and political indicators of future defeat for reelection of incumbent school board members.[5] It was hoped that if such indicators could be discovered (see appendix 6A for specific indicators), then unnecessary political conflict within school districts could be avoided. Community leaders might be alerted in advance to the necessity of changing programs and policies to meet emerging needs.

Of the southern California school districts previously studied 37 were included in the research. In 19 of the districts, no incumbent school board member had suffered defeat in a board election between 1952 and 1965. These districts were randomly selected. They were compared with 18 school districts, all the districts in the four counties in which an incumbent had been defeated in the 1961 election and in which the superintendency changed. (in 8 of the districts, no incumbent experienced defeat between 1952 and 1961; in 10, there had been one or more incumbent defeats during that time.)

Three common descriptive characteristics of school districts were used in the study: (1) average daily attendance, (2) assessed valuation, and (3) number of votes cast for each candidate at school board elections. These characteristics represent data readily available to school boards and superintendents. Such data also may be representative of significant changes occurring within a given school district.

Average daily attendance indicates the size of a school district. Increases or decreases in average daily attendance represent changes in needs for staffing and facilities. Changes in average daily attendance also may reflect changes in land use as well as provide some indications of changes in population density, the average number of school-age children per capita, and the ratio of the number of children attending public schools to the number attending private and parochial schools. Significant shifts in any of these have meaning for the educational values of a community.

Assessed valuation of property is a measure of the gross wealth of the school district. It is an indication of the district's financial capacity to meet the stress of changing programs. Changes in assessed valuation reflect changes in land use and assessment practice. These also reflect socioeconomic conditions within a community. Assessed valuation per child in average daily attendance is even a stronger indication of the ability of a community to support its schools. Changes in assessed valuation per child in average daily attendance are probably good indicators of new building and change in land use, therefore suggesting changes in the social class composition of a school district's population.

Generally, school board elections provide models of voter apathy. In the four counties studied, the vast majority of school boards were elected by small minorities of eligible voters. Small voter turnout is in part a reflection of the lack of organized opposition to the policies of the establishment. It was hypothesized that as a significant increase in ballots cast in a board of education election resulted in a higher ratio of votes against incumbents, it would precede the actual defeat of an incumbent.

A number of analyses were made of these data. Briefly, antecedent events to the defeats of incumbent board members in 1961 were revealed. The strongest predictors were (1) the percentage change in assessed valuation over the 3-year period 1951-1952 to 1954-1955, (2) the percentage change in average daily attendance over the 3-year period 1956-1957 to 1959-1960, and (3) the ratio of votes against incumbents to total votes cast in the 1959 election. The change in assessed valuation occured some eight years prior to the significant political shift in voting behavior.

Summary

The three studies briefly summarized above provide support for the theory of political change outlined earlier in the chapter. Social and economic changes in a given community will be reflected in changes in the community's value structure. If the established order cannot adjust or change in response to changing needs and values in its community, then political action to bring about the desired changes will result. In the school district, incumbent defeat is the signal that a political shift is taking place. More often than not the superintendent has identified with the policies of the old regime and is vulnerable in such a circumstance. In all probability there will be a change in chief school officers following incumbent defeat of a school board member. When a new superintendent sits with the new school board, he or she will represent a different value orientation than did his or her predecessor.

The research summarized in this chapter reflects a period in the politics of local school districts in which political conflict was an exception. The politics of local school districts could be characterized as having long periods of stability, with occasional periods of instability, signaling an adjustment within the decision-making structure to bring it more into line with socioeconomic conditions and value structure in the school district. There is no law which requires that there be long periods of political stability within a school district. School districts are not isolated from the larger society. It is clear that school boards and superintendents must and will respond to pressures not only from within their systems but also from without. Political instability already has become a way of life in some school districts. Whether this is merely the high-conflict period for these districts or whether in the future local school districts will experience more periods of political strife than did school districts in the past is not clear at this time.

32

Notes

1. John C. Walden, "School Board Changes and Involuntary Superintendent Turnover," unpublished Ph.D. dissertation, Claremont Graduate School, Claremont, Calif., 1966, pp. 21-22. See also Laurence Iannaccone and Frank W. Lutz, *Politics, Power and Policy: The Governing of Local School Districts* (Columbus, Ohio: Charles E. Merrill, 1970), p. 97.

2. Gladys M. Kammerer et al., *The Urban Political Community: Profiles in Town Politics* (Boston: Houghton Mifflin, 1963).

3. Ibid.

4. Robert M. Freeborn, "School Board Changes and the Succession Patterns of Superintendents," unpublished Ph.D. dissertation, Claremont Graduate School, Claremont, Calif., 1966.

5. Richard S. Kirkendall, "Discriminating Social Economic and Political Characteristics of Changing versus Stable Policy-Making Systems in School Districts," unpublished Ph.D. dissertation, Claremont Graduate School, Claremont, Calif., 1966. See also the discussion of this study in Iannaccone and Lutz, *Politics, Power and Policy*, pp. 96-103, from which much of the balance of this chapter is drawn.

4

The Effect of Partisan Election on the Relationship between Incumbent Defeat and Superintendent Turnover

Allen W. Moen

Introduction

Until recently the governance of public education was popularly thought of as separate from the political process. More and more, however, the governance of public education is recognized as a political process. While the association between educational governance and the political process is being accepted, the nature and the extent of the relationship are far from fully understood. If the governance of public education is a political process, is it subject to the same political pressures as is the governance of the city or town? Does the fact that school board members are generally not elected on a partisan basis make them less political creatures than other types of candidates endorsed as a Republican, Democrat, or other party member? Are school board members who are elected on a partisan basis more political than school board members who have not been elected on a partisan basis? Finally, what is the effect of the political activity exhibited by school board members upon the superintendent serving the board of education made up of these elected school board members?

Previous chapters have established the political nature of educational governance. However, the research reported was undertaken in situations not providing for the partisan election of school board members. In those studies school board elections were observed in states not having partisan election of school board members. The research reported in this chapter[1] was conducted in Pennsylvania, a state in which candidates for the school board must declare their party and run on a partisan ticket,[2] although it is possible for a school board candidate to cross-file and run on both tickets. Thus, if partisanship is an ingredient of political activity, the school board elections in Pennsylvania may be even more political than those found in many other states. In conducting the research, we were interested in studying the effect of the partisan nature of the election upon incumbent school board member defeat and the turnover of superintendents in such districts. Do school boards elected on a partisan basis reflect more accurately the needs and wishes of residents of the district than do boards not elected on a partisan basis? Does electing boards on a partisan basis make them more responsive to the demands of the constituency? If this is the case, it would seem that states electing school board members on a partisan basis would demonstrate a relationship between incumbent school board member defeat and superintendent turnover different from that of states electing their board members on a nonpartisan basis.

33

Theoretical Background

An abundance of literature reveals that a great deal of power in educational decision making rests with local school boards. The amount of power residing with the board may vary. In the small communities of the Springdale studies by Vidich and Bensman[3] and Central Forks studied by Goldhammer,[4] it was observed that the central leadership group in the community held many of the positions on the school board. This phenomenon was contrasted in Hunter's regional city[5] where school board membership and educational policy determination were left to the "lower limits power personnel." However, in most communities, the power exercised by the school board has been viewed as nonpolitical. If political activity need be equated with partisanship, there is often, in fact, a lack of political activity at the school board level. However, political activity can exist outside the sphere of partisanship. Although the term *politics* as popularly used has rather negative connotations, a closer look displays how closely politics is tied in with the governance of school districts. Robert Dahl has defined politics as "the authoritative allocation of values."[6] Lutz and Iannaccone view politics as "the process of influence which results in an authoritative decision, having the force of law, by a governmental body such as a school board."[7] A third dimension is developed by Thomas Eliot when he says that "politics includes the making of governmental decisions, and the effort or struggle to gain or keep the power to make these decisions."[8] If the preceding are definitions of the term *politics,* they most certainly relate also to governance of public education. Thus, we find school board members directly involved as politicians in the governance of their school districts. They represent and respond to a constituency just as any other political being does.

Research reported in earlier chapters has established the relationship between the political turnover of members of school boards and the subsequent involuntary turnover of superintendents in those districts experiencing board member termination. These studies have found that school board member defeat indicates a lack of satisfaction by the constituency of these board members in the operation of the schools. Furthermore, this lack of satisfaction has frequently culminated in the involuntary termination of the superintendent's contract. The work of Lutz, Walden, Kirkendall, and Freeborn[9] was conducted in states in which school board members are elected on a nonpartisan basis. Would a school board elected on a partisan basis more adequately and perhaps more concurrently reflect the wishes of the constituency? Would it follow, therefore, that the subsequent termination of the superintendent would be affected by the partisan nature of the election of board members?

A second area of research involving partisan elections was also instrumental in developing the theoretical basis of this study. Many studies have shown voting behavior in America to be quite predictable. Certain forces act upon voters in determining how they will vote. The most powerful of these forces is the voter's party identification. It has been estimated that about 75 percent of the electorate identify to some degree with either the Democratic or Republican parties. The majority of these party identifiers say they have regularly voted for the nominee of their party.[10]

Thus, it has been established that school district governance is a political activity. Often school board members do respond to a constituency. Furthermore, on the basis of an abundance of research in political science, a relationship has been found to exist between the party identification of a voter and that voter's behavior in the voting booth. It was expected that such voter behavior would be exhibited in voting in school board elections as well.

The Hypotheses

Specifically, the objective of this study was to determine the relationship between the electoral defeat of an incumbent school board member and any subsequent involuntary turnover in the superintendency in that school district, as well as the degree and manner in which the partisan nature of the school board election influenced that relationship.

The hypotheses guiding this study were as follows:

1. In partisan general elections in Pennsylvania, more school board candidates win when their party wins than when their party loses.
2. The defeat of an incumbent school board member in Pennsylvania's partisan general election does not necessarily reflect community dissatisfaction with the school board and its policy to the degree that involuntary superintendent turnover does.
   (a) The defeat of a renominated, incumbent school board member accompanied by the defeat of the rest of the incumbent's party will not signal involuntary superintendent turnover within 3 years.
   (b) The defeat of an incumbent school board member in a party primary election will signal involuntary superintendent turnover within 3 years.
   (c) The defeat of a renominated incumbent school board member in the partisan general election accompanied by a victory of the rest of the incumbent's party will be the strongest indicator of involuntary superintendent turnover within 3 years.

Hypothesis 1 suggested that the success of a candidate in a school board election depended upon the success of that candidate's party. That is, school board candidates will win more often when the rest of their party wins than when the rest of their party loses. A second hypothesis guiding the study was that the defeat of an incumbent school board member under varying conditions predicted superintendent turnover with differing degrees of accuracy. Defeat in the general election might possibly be indicative of future involuntary turnover in the superintendent's office. Hypotheses 2(*a*) and (*c*) distinguished two categories of incumbent defeat in the general election. In hypothesis 2(*a*), it was hypothesized that the defeat of an incumbent in the general election accompanied by the defeat of the incumbent's party would not be a significant predictor of superintendent turnover. Rather, it was simply a matter of one party's being turned out for another. This phenomenon was closely related to hypothesis 1 in which it was predicted that a candidate's success went hand in hand with party success. Hypothesis 2(*c*) observed the defeat of an incumbent school board member in the general election in which the remainder of the incumbent's party enjoyed victory. This defeat, it was hypothesized, would be the most accurate indicator of involuntary superintendent turnover of any electoral defeat studied. This type of defeat was anticipated to be the strongest indication that the policies of that incumbent were not viewed with favor by the public. The tendency to vote for candidates of the same party was overcome by this strong distaste for the policies of a particular incumbent candidate.

Hypothesis 2(*b*) identified a third category of incumbent defeat—the defeat of the incumbent school board member in his/her party's primary election. It hypothesized that incumbent defeat in this election would predict superintendent turnover although not as accurately as the defeat described in hypothesis 2(*c*). It was felt that the absence of partisan politics in the primary election would focus attention on educational issues. Thus, defeat would represent repudiation of educational policies supported by the superintendent and implemented by the board.

Research Procedures

The study was set in 192 Pennsylvania school districts. Each district was governed by a nine-member school board with the power to hire and fire the superintendent. Three of the nine members on each board were elected to 6-year terms each odd-numbered year. These elections were held coincidentally with other local elections. In 1967, the general elections were held on November 7, and the new board held its organizational meeting on December 4. Pennsylvania school board directors are elected in partisan contests. To obtain a position on the November ballot, the candidate must have first secured his or her party's nomination in the spring primary election held on May 16, 1967. Thus, Pennsylvania school board incumbents twice face the danger of defeat in their quest for reelection.

All districts in the sample had superintendents as their chief school administrators rather than supervising principals who reported to a county superintendent of schools. The superintendent was independent of the county superintendent and operated on a 4-year contract. The 4-year contracts of all superintendents begin and expire on the same date, July 1, of every fourth year.

Thus, the contract period examined in this study originated on July 1, 1966, the date that all superintendents signed their 4-year contracts. These contracts came up for renewal on July 1, 1970. During this 4-year period, the contracts could not be extended but could be terminated. All superintendents are elected in April, but the contract period does not begin until July 1.

This study, then, examined the election of 1967 and the 3-year period following it. The first opportunity for incumbent school board defeat in 1967 was the May primary election. The general election was held in November, at which time composition of the new board was determined. But the new board did not meet and organize itself until December 4, 1967. It was at this point that the 3-year period began during which superintendent turnover could be explained by incumbent school board member defeat occurring in 1967. This study, therefore, was concerned with explaining involuntary superintendent turnover occurring between December 4, 1967, and December 4, 1970. This span of time included July 1, 1970, the date on which all superintendents of Pennsylvania signed contracts if they were to retain their position for another 4-year period. It was anticipated that most of the superintendency turnovers would take place at this time.

Collection of Data

In order to test hypothesis 1, victory was operationally defined as the party whose candidates were elected or received a majority of the vote in more than one-half of all contests appearing on the ballot in that school district. Data regarding election results were collected from local newspaper accounts of the election. Where local newspapers did not carry the election results, the necessary information was secured via telephone calls to the school district. Data related to superintendent turnover were obtained at the Pennsylvania State Department of Education. For the purposes of this study, it was necessary to determine if the superintendency turnover was of a voluntary or an involuntary nature. It was decided that this information could be obtained most adequately through a questionnaire completed by the successor superintendent. Questionnaires were sent to successor superintendents. In the case of unreturned questionnaires, the appropriate district was contacted by telephone. Thus, a response was obtained from all successor superintendents in districts in which superintendent turnover had occurred during the period of the study.

Data Analysis

Chi square was selected as the statistical procedure to be used in testing the significance of the relationship between incumbent school board member defeat and involuntary superintendent turnover. A 2 × 2 contingency table utilizing the

Yates chi square correction was employed. A probability of .05 was selected as the level of significance necessary in order to reject the null hypothesis. In testing hypothesis 1, usable data were available from 192 districts; and hypotheses 2, 2(a), 2 (b), and 2(c) were tested with data drawn from 165 districts. Districts were randomly selected with regard to size categories, urban-rural location, and geographical distribution within the state.

Hypothesis 1 stated that in partisan, general elections in Pennsylvania, more school board candidates win when their party wins than when their party loses. Table 4-1 presents the data concerning the relationship between individual and party success or failure. The data strongly support hypothesis 1.

Hypothesis 2 declared that the defeat of an incumbent school board member in Pennsylvania's partisan general election does not necessarily reflect community dissatisfaction with the school board and its policy to the degree that involuntary superintendent turnover does.

Again, the hypothesis was supported by the data. Chi square analysis failed to identify a significant relationship between the defeat of an incumbent school board member in the general election and involuntary superintendent turnover at the .05 level of significance. However, a refinement of hypothesis 2 did result in obtaining a level of significance. Inasmuch as victory in the party primary was necessary to be eligible for competition at the general election level, all participants in the general election had already survived one potential defeat. Candidates in the general election had already been victorious in the party's primary election. Voters in these districts had had the opportunity to defeat incumbents with whom they associated unpopular educational policies. Thus, it followed that voters in those districts in which incumbent defeat had occurred in the spring primary had voiced their opposition to existing board policy, and further incumbent defeat in the general election was not necessary to express that opposition. Under the terms of this study, the superintendent was already eligible to be dismissed. However, in those districts in which incumbent primary defeat had not taken place, the voters had retained the opportunity to defeat

Table 4-1

Candidate Victory-Candidate Defeat versus Candidate's Party Victory-Candidate's Party Defeat

| Party | Candidate | | Total |
	Wins	Loses	
Wins	775	132	907
Loses	132	775	907
Total	907	907	$N = 1814$

$X^2 = 908.8; X^2 \ (.001) = 10.83$

incumbent board members in the general election, and in so doing expressed their dissatisfaction with board policy. There were 102 districts in which incumbents had not suffered defeat in the primary election. The relationship between the two variables in these districts were subjected to chi square analysis. The chi square obtained was 4.64 and was significant at the .05 level of probability.

The relationship between incumbent defeat in the general election and involuntary superintendent turnover was further strengthened in those districts in which primary defeat had not occurred when data from only those districts which experienced subsequent superintendent turnover were examined. There were 39 districts in this category; the chi square was 6.64, which was significant at the .01 level.

Hypothesis 2(*a*) stated that the defeat of a renominated, incumbent school board member accompanied by the defeat of the rest of the incumbent's party will not signal involuntary superintendent turnover within 3 years.

Again, the data supported the hypothesis. No significant relationship was found between the defeat of an incumbent board member in the general election at the same time that the incumbent's party was being defeated and subsequent superintendent dismissal. Likewise, a significant relationship was not found by examining only those districts in which superintendent dismissal was eventually experienced.

Hypothesis 2(*b*) stated that the defeat of an incumbent school board member in a primary election will signal involuntary superintendent turnover within 3 years. There were 163 districts in this category. Analysis of the data produced a chi square of 4.77, significant at the .05 level of probability, demonstrating the relationship between incumbent defeat in the primary election and subsequent superintendent dismissal.

The relationship between incumbent defeat in the primary election and involuntary superintendent turnover was determined to be of greater statistical significance when only those districts that went on to experience superintendent turnover were examined. The chi square was 7.72, significant at the .01 level.

In hypothesis 2(*c*) it was posited that the defeat of a renominated incumbent school board member in the partisan general election accompanied by the defeat of the rest of the incumbent's party will be the strongest indicator of involuntary superintendent turnover within 3 years. Analysis of the data resulted in a rejection of this hypothesis. No significant relationship was found between the two variables.

Ancillary Findings

Perhaps the most noteworthy finding of the study was not the result of the testing of any of the above hypotheses. As the data were collected, it became evident that another independent variable should have been developed in explaining superintendent turnover. In the newly created hypotheses, all references to the partisan nature of the election including categories of incumbent defeat (such as individual defeat accompanied by party victory or individual defeat accompanied by party defeat) were omitted. The hypothesis tested the relationship between simple incumbent defeat—regardless of other partisan victories or defeats—and superintendent turnover. This relationship is examined in table 4-2. It will be noted that a relationship significant beyond the .01 level was found in observing this relationship.

Discussion

Prior to the examination of the data collected for this study, it was expected that the defeat of an incumbent school board member in the general election accompanied by the victory of his/her party in that election would be a very positive signal of upcoming incumbent superintendent involuntary turnover. It was expected that other antecedents to superintendent turnover would also be identified. It was hypothesized that incumbent school board member defeat in the primary election would be a strong indicator of upcoming superintendent turnover as well. Furthermore, it was anticipated that the defeat of a school board member accompanied by the defeat of the rest of the party would have little bearing on the status of the incumbent superintendent.

As the data in the study were analyzed, it became apparent that the defeat of an incumbent board member in the general election accompanied by the victory of the incumbent's party was not a strong indicator of future superintendent turnover. In fact, no significant relationship was established between the two variables. Likewise, the incumbent's defeat accompanied by the defeat of the party was not found to be a forerunner of superintendent turnover. It was found, however, that incumbent school board member defeat in the primary election was a strong predictor of future superintendent involuntary turnover. In

Table 4-2
Total Involuntary Turnover-No Involuntary Turnover versus Incumbent Defeat-No Incumbent Defeat in the Primary and General Elections

Incumbent Defeat[a]	Involuntary Turnover		Total
	Yes	No	
Yes	29	64	93
No	7	61	68
Total	36	125	$N = 161$

$X^2 = 9.60; X^2 (.01) = 6.64$

addition, the ancillary finding of this study was that incumbent defeat, an inclusive category not divided into any subgrouping, was in fact the most significant predictor examined.

The benefit of hindsight enables the researcher to explain the phenomena discovered in the study. A party primary election in many ways resembles a nonpartisan general election. In a primary election, the partisan factor is eliminated as completely as is possible in a partisan setting. In Pennsylvania only registered party members may vote in their party's primary election. As much as is possible, the individual candidate is evaluated in the primary election. There is little relationship to partisan activity other than the basic requirement that the voters claim membership in the same party as the candidate for whom they are voting. In voting in the Republican or Democratic primary, a Republican or Democratic voter theoretically reviews the qualities of the individual candidate. A similar phenomenon is demonstrated by the behavior of voters in nonpartisan general elections. The voters are viewing the individual candidate's strengths and weaknesses without regard to the party to which they may happen to belong. States in which school board members are not elected on a partisan basis generally do not have primary elections previous to the general election. Thus, both the primary election in states with partisan elections and the general election in states without partisan activity provide the voters with their first opportunity to evaluate incumbent candidates for office. Defeat in the primary election in a partisan election represents the first opportunity for the voter to eliminate an unwanted incumbent, just as does the defeat of the incumbent in general and nonpartisan elections. Thus, the significance of the relationship between partisan defeat in a primary election and subsequent nonvoluntary superintendent turnover need not be interpreted to be influenced by the partisan nature of the election. Rather it merely represents the first opportunity for dissatisfied voters and district residents to initiate the process leading to the dismissal of the superintendent. The occurrence of the defeat within the context of partisan activity has very little effect on the relationship to future superintendent turnover. The incidence of incumbent defeat is the pervasive factor.

It is interesting to note that more than half of all incumbent defeats observed in this study took place in the primary election. This would seem to indicate that if there is dissatisfaction with the incumbent school board member, the chances are good that he/she will be eliminated at the first opportunity by the voters.

Thus, this study substantiates but differs little from the findings reported earlier in the book. The defeat of incumbents in the first opportunity provided to voters signaled involuntary superintendent turnover. The present study observed the same phenomenon. Additionally it was discovered in this study that simple incumbent school board member defeat regardless of the circumstances within which the defeat occurred is the best single predictor of superintendent turnover. It is a better predictor than incumbent defeat in a general election accompanied by the victory of the party; it is a better predictor than the defeat of an incumbent in a general election accompanied by the party's defeat; and it is a better predictor than defeat of an incumbent in a primary election. Furthermore, when only districts experiencing superintendent turnover were analyzed, the relationship between incumbent defeat and involuntary turnover increased to a significance level of .001. This level of significance matched that found in the original work studying nonpartisan elections. This would indicate that inasmuch as the relationship found in this study was similar to the relationship between the two variables established in nonpartisan election studies, the relationship was affected very little by the partisan nature of the school board elections in Pennsylvania.

Summary

Analysis of the data collected in this study revealed that incumbent defeat, when broadly defined as the defeat of an incumbent in either the primary or general elections, is the most accurate predictor of involuntary superintendent turnover. Increased predictive accuracy cannot be obtained by examining any specific category of incumbent defeat as a result of partisan elections. Thus, the findings of previous studies taking place in nonpartisan school board elections were found to be equally applicable in partisan school district politics. Nothing in the present study indicated that the relationship between incumbent school board member defeat and involuntary superintendent turnover is influenced by the partisan nature of Pennsylvania school board elections.

Notes

1. Allen W. Moen, "Superintendent Turnover as Predicted by School Board Incumbent Defeat in Pennsylvania's Partisan Elections," unpublished Ph.D. dissertation, Pennsylvania State University, 1971.

2. Barry O. Miller, "Effects of Cross-Filing on School Board Incumbents in Pennsylvania's Elections," unpublished Ph.D. dissertation, The Pennsylvania State University, 1975.

3. Arthur J. Vidich and Joseph Bensman, *Small Town in Mass Society*, rev. ed. (Princeton, N.J.: Princeton University Press, 1968).

4. Keith Goldhammer, *The School Board* (New York: The Center for Applied Research in Education, Inc., 1964).

5. Floyd Hunter, *Community Power Structure* (Chapel Hill: University of North Carolina Press, 1953).

6. Robert A. Dahl, *Modern Political Analysis* (Englewood Cliffs, N.J.: Prentice-Hall, Inc., 1963).

7. Frank W. Lutz and Laurence Iannaccone, *Understanding Educational Organizations, A Field Study Approach* (Columbus, Ohio: Charles E. Merrill Publishing Company, 1969).

8. Thomas H. Eliot, "Toward an Understanding of Public School Politics," *American Political Science Review*, vol. 53, no. 4 (December 1959), pp. 1032-52.

9. Robert M. Freeborn, "School Board Changes and the Succession Patterns of Superintendents," unpublished Ph.D. dissertation, Claremont Graduate School, 1966.

Richard S. Kirkendall, "Discriminating Social, Economic, and Political Characteristics of Changing Versus Stable Policy-Making Systems in School Districts," unpublished Ph.D. dissertation, Claremont Graduate School, 1966.

Frank W. Lutz, "Social Systems and School Districts," unpublished Ed.D. dissertation, Washington University, St. Louis, 1962.

John C. Walden, "School Board Changes and Involuntary Superintendent Turnover," unpublished Ph.D. dissertation, Claremont Graduate School and University Center, 1966.

10. Fred I. Greenstein, *The American Party System and the American People*, 2d ed. (Englewood Cliffs, N.J.: Prentice-Hall, Inc., 1970).

Downward Trends in Socioeconomic-Political Indicators and Incumbent Defeat

Martin Burlingame

Earlier writings have explored the general applicability of the Iannaccone-Lutz framework to a nonrandom sample of 66 of New Mexico's 89 school districts.[1] As was the case in most states, a review of the school enrollment figures and general census materials for New Mexico indicated considerable population mobility. Of the 66 districts in the sample, 41 had declining school enrollments in the 1960s. A review of the 1970 census for New Mexico showed that total population had declined in 17 of the state's 32 counties. In 14 predominantly rural counties this population loss was 5 percent or more. In incorporated places of 1000 or more inhabitants, 21 lost 5 percent or more of their population while 17 had a 5 percent or more increase. Generally, larger cities increased while smaller towns or villages lost inhabitants. Such a pattern of mobility paralleled the national experience in which roughly half of all counties lost population in the 1960s.

The general intent of this chapter is an exploration of the relation of declining socioeconomic-political indicators and incumbent defeat. This exploration proceeds as follows: first, an examination is made of the total sample of 66 districts using groups created from the increase or decrease in indicator variables *and* board member defeats in 1967, 1969, and 1971 school board elections; second, an examination is made of two groups, 44 districts and 22 districts, using new decision rules concerning incumbents not seeking reelection *and* 1971 elections only; third, there is a discussion of the results of these analyses.

The Analyses of 66 Districts

The initial data analyses were based on the entire sample of 66 school districts. The districts were grouped on the basis of (1) increase *or* decrease in indicator variables and (2) no board member defeat *or* one or more board member defeats in the 1967, 1969, and 1971 school board elections. In the case of a decrease in indicators, the decision rule employed was that a negative sign in the raw score of any two or more of the 11 socioeconomic indicators of a district constituted grounds for assignment as a decreasing indicator district. (Indicator variables are listed in appendixes 6A and 6B.) Overall, 41 districts were designated as decreasing indicator districts, and 25 districts were assigned to increasing categories. In the case of board member defeat, districts in which incumbents did not seek reelection were assigned to categories of no board member defeat. Under this decision rule, 36 districts were assigned to no-defeat categories. The exact number and the fourfold classifications are presented in figure 5-1.

66 Districts, 19 Indicators

The predictability rates for classifying the 66 districts into the four groups had a mean of 63 percent. The results are presented in table 5-1. Inspection of the table indicates that misclassifications occurred most frequently in group 2 (increasing indicators, board member defeat), but group 4 districts (decreasing indicators, board member defeat) were as frequently misclassified as group 2 districts. Therefore, no unique clusters, such as increasing or decreasing indicator groups regardless of classification of board member defeats, could be found.

66 Districts, 10 Indicators

By using those variables with the largest discriminant function coefficients, a second analysis was performed. While the mean of the predictability rates was 60 percent, there were shifts in some classifications. Group 1 had one more district correctly classified while group 2 lost three districts which had previously been correctly classified. Again, no clustering, such as increase in indicators or board member defeats, seems to have occurred.

The indicator variables included all four concerning change in average daily membership (1, 2, 3, 4), two involving changes in assessed valuation per average

Group 1	Group 2
(1) Increase in indicator variables *and*	(1) Increase in indicator variables *and*
(2) No board member defeat N = 10	(2) Board member defeat N = 15
Group 3	Group 4
(1) Decrease in some indicator variables *and*	(1) Decreases in some indicator variables *and*
(2) No board member defeat N = 26	(2) Board member defeat N = 15

Figure 5-1. Predicted Groups Created to Examine the Effects of a Decrease in Some Indicators for 1967, 1969, and 1971 School Board Elections

Table 5-1
Classification Matrix of 66 Districts Using 19 Indicators

Group	1	2	3	4	Total	Predictability Rate, %
1	6	3	1	0	10	60
2	2	10	1	2	15	67
3	1	1	17	7	26	65
4	0	4	2	9	15	60

Mean Predictability Rate: 63 percent

daily membership (10, 11), and four political variables including ratio of votes against incumbents, ratio of candidates, incumbent, index, and board election index (12, 13, 17, 19).

66 Districts, 5 Indicators

The final analysis reported used five indicators and resulted in a mean predictability rate of 48 percent. While groups 1 and 4 fell dramatically from earlier analyses, only group 3 (decreasing indicators, no board member defeat) remained stable over all three analyses. The indicator variables in this analysis dealt with change in average daily membership (1, 3, 4) and votes against incumbents (12, 13).

Summary

These three analyses produced neither high levels of predictability nor patterns which seemed to lead to further analyses. Combining classifications and misclassifications of increasing indicators, for example, did not produce striking patterns which might have aided further analysis. The indicator variables suggested that changes in average daily membership and voting patterns might be useful as predictors for some groups, but not all.

The Analyses of 44 and 22 Districts

At this time, a second series of analyses were run. These analyses were based on changing the decision rules used for classifying districts.

The first change was of the decision rule concerning incumbents who did not seek reelection. An inspection of the data generated showed that in the 1971 school board elections, some 22 districts had at least one incumbent candidate who did not seek reelection. According to information published by the New Mexico School Boards Association, 173 of the 453 local school board positions (38.2 percent) were open for election in 1971. Of the 89 school districts in New Mexico at that time, 77 had two or more school board positions up for election. Hence, two analysis series were run using districts in which all incumbents had sought reelection ($N = 44$) and districts in which at least one incumbent did not seek reelection ($N = 22$).

The second change was to analyze only the results of 1971 school board elections. These two changes in decision rules produced the following analyses.

44 Districts—19, 11, and 4 Indicators

The first series of analyses used two groups. Using only 1971 election information, group 1 included all districts in which incumbents sought reelection and none were defeated ($N = 30$); group 2 included all districts in which incumbents sought reelection but one or more were defeated ($N = 14$).

Using all 19 indicator variables, the mean predictability rate was 95 percent. Only 2 of the 44 districts were not classified correctly. However, with 11 indicators predictability rates fell to a 71 percent mean, and with 5 indicators predictability rates fell to 57 percent. In the 11-indicator analysis, 7 were socioeconomic (1, 2, 3, 5, 6, 10, 11) and 4 political (13, 15, 17, 19). In the 5-indicator analysis, all were socioeconomic (1, 7, 8, 10, 11).

22 Districts, 19 Indicators

By using all districts in which at least one incumbent did not seek reelection, four groups were created. These groups were classified on the dimensions of (1) increase or decrease in indicator variables and (2) no board member defeat or at least one board member defeat. The groups and the number of districts in each are displayed in figure 5-2. The predictability rate for these four groups, using all 19 variables, was 100 percent.

22 Districts, 10 Indicators

Using the ten largest discriminant function coefficients, a second analysis was performed. Again, the predictability rate for all four groups was 100 percent. Of the indicator variables used, 8 were socioeconomic (1, 2, 3, 4, 5, 6, 10, 11) and 2 were political (12, 13).

Group 1	Group 2
(1) Increase in indicator variables *and*	(1) Increase in indicator variables *and*
(2) No board member defeat *and*	(2) At least one board member defeat *and*
(3) Incumbent not candidate for reelection in 1971 $N = 4$	(3) Incumbent not candidate for reelection in 1971 $N = 2$
Group 3	Group 4
(1) Decrease in some indicator variables *and*	(1) Decrease in some indicator variables *and*
(2) No board member defeat *and*	(2) At least one board member defeat *and*
(3) Incumbent not candidate for reelection in 1971 $N = 14$	(3) Incumbent not candidate for reelection in 1971 $N = 2$

Figure 5-2. Predicted Groups Created to Examine the Effects of Decrease in Some Indicators When Incumbent Is Not Seeking Reelection in 1971 School Board Election

22 Districts, 5 Indicators

The final analysis used 3 socioeconomic variables (1, 2, 4) and 2 political variables (12, 13). The mean predictability rate was 87 percent. Misclassifications occurred in groups 1 and 3.

Summary

By changing the decision rules concerning incumbents not seeking reelection and by using only a single election year (1971), mean predictability rates were generally higher than in earlier analyses. The next section explores the possible reasons for these increases.

Discussion

This section presents one possible interpretation of the earlier sets of analyses. This interpretation rests upon the analyses of the 1971 school board election in the 44 districts in which all incumbents sought reelection and the 22 districts in which at least one incumbent did not seek reelection. Two major points will be stressed. First, there are different patterns of indicators in the 44- and 22-district analyses. Second, in the 1971 elections there was considerable turnover of school board members.

Incumbents Not Seeking Reelection

The use of the decision rule which reclassified districts in terms of incumbent choices of seeking or not seeking reelection in 1971 produced two major results. First, predictability rates were generally higher than those associated for the total sample. Second, a pattern of indicators emerged in analyses run with less than all 19 indicators. This pattern is most evident in the analysis using 10- and 11-indicator variables. This pattern included eight common indicator variables and a few unique variables. The information is displayed in table 5-2.

Table 5-2
Summary of Indicators Retained in Classification of Districts Using Incumbent Reelection and 1971 Rules

Number of Districts	44	22
Indicators	11	10
Mean Predictability Rates	71%	100%
Number of Groups	2	4
Indicators		
1	a	a
2	a	a
3	a	a
4		a
5	a	a
6	a	a
7		
8		
9		
10	a	a
11	a	a
12		a
13	a	a
14		
15	a	
16		
17	a	
18		
19	a	

aRetained.

The common indicator variables retained in both analyses were 1, 2, 3, 5, 6, 10, 11, 12, 13. These eight variables included three concerning percent change in average daily membership (1, 2, 3), two dealing with percent change in assessed valuation (5, 6), two covering the percent change in assessed valuation per average daily membership (10, 11), and one reflecting a ratio of votes against incumbents to total votes in the 1967 board election (13). In the 44-district classification, the unique variables were 15, 17, and 19. These variables dealt with the ratio of candidates to positions in the 1969 election (15), an incumbent index for the 1967 election (17), and a board election index for the 1967 election (19). In the 22-district classification, the unique variables were 4 and 12. The first indicator (4) was the percent change in average daily membership over the 8-year period from 1961-1962 to 1969-1970, and the second indicator (12) was the ratio of votes against incumbents to total votes in the 1969 board election.

The groupings of these indicator variables suggest a picture of generalized changes in districts on common socioeconomic dimensions but sharply differing interpretations by school board incumbents of political changes. In the 44-district sample, three political indicators remain. These indicators helped discriminate between districts in which defeat or no defeat took place in 1971. There were no unique political indicators in the 22-district sample. Such political indicators were not useful for discriminating districts in which incumbents either won or lost in 1971.

In the 1971 election, 18 districts had incumbent defeat. In the 44-district sample, 32 percent (14/44) of the districts had at least one incumbent defeat. In the smaller sample, 18 percent (4/22) suffered defeat. The actual number of defeats and the percentage difference between the two samples are large.

What these differences in political indicators and actual political outcomes may indicate is that the decision to *not* seek reelection may have been based on an accurate assessment of a changing political scene. Those incumbents who did not seek reelection were aware of and understood earlier political indicators (15, 17, 19) as symptoms of high probability of defeat. In those 22 districts in which incumbents did not seek reelection, these and other political clues had already been analyzed by incumbents, and formed the basis for political retirement. The decision rule to separate out incumbents not seeking reelection thus included these political variables as a common, and nondiscriminating, factor.

In the 44 districts in which all incumbents sought reelection, early political variables helped discriminate between incumbent victory and defeat. Incumbents in these districts may not have been aware of or may have misinterpreted the political process (15, 17, 19). Hence, those who suffered defeat could be correctly classified using earlier political signals. The decision rule to exclude incumbents not seeking reelection in these 44 districts thus reintroduced the political variables. The interpretation suggested is presented schematically in figure 5-3.

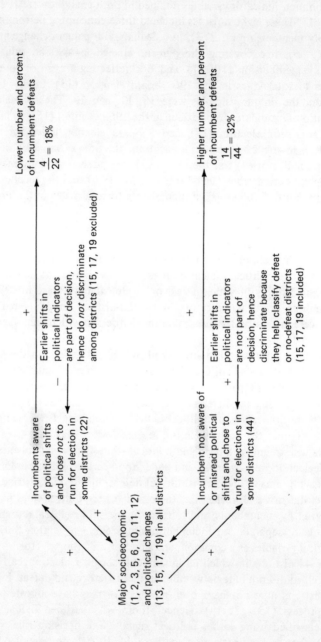

Major socioeconomic
(1, 2, 3, 5, 6, 10, 11, 12)
and political changes
(13, 15, 17, 19) in all districts

Incumbents aware
of political shifts
and chose *not* to
run for election in
some districts (22)

Earlier shifts in
political indicators
are part of decision,
hence do *not* discriminate
among districts (15, 17, 19 excluded)

Lower number and percent
of incumbent defeats

$$\frac{4}{22} = 18\%$$

Incumbent not aware of
or misread political
shifts and chose to
run for elections in
some districts (44)

Earlier shifts in
political indicators
are not part of
decision, hence
discriminate because
they help classify defeat
or no-defeat districts
(15, 17, 19 included)

Higher number and percent
of incumbent defeats

$$\frac{14}{44} = 32\%$$

Figure 5-3. Schematic Interpretation

High Turnover

In the sample of 66 districts, some incumbent change (defeat or not seeking reelection) occurred in 36 districts (55 percent) in 1971. In 14 (21 percent) of the districts, incumbents ran and lost. In 4 districts some incumbents ran and lost, and other incumbents did not seek reelection (6 percent). In 18 districts (27 percent) incumbents did not seek reelection.

Summary

The sense which can be drawn from these two points suggests that school board members in some districts were alert to major political shifts which were occurring in their school districts. In other districts, other incumbents suffered defeat nearly twice as often as their more alert counterparts. More importantly, however, in 1971 the majority of this sample was made up of districts in which at least one member of the school board changed. This rate of mobility suggests that boards may have been open both to their community and to potentially new demands on the schools. These two points suggest that in 1971 in New Mexico a close link between school and community existed in a majority of districts of this sample.

Note

1. In the interest of avoiding needless repetition, for the theoretical framework, readers should refer to Laurence Iannaccone and Frank W. Lutz, *Politics, Power and Policy: The Governing of Local School Districts.* The particular work in New Mexico was Eugene P. LeDoux, "Outmigration: Its Relation to Social, Political and Economic Conditions and to the Governing of Local School Districts in New Mexico," unpublished Ph.D. dissertation, University of New Mexico, 1971). Material from this dissertation was used in Eugene P. LeDoux and Martin Burlingame, "The Iannaccone-Lutz Model of School Board Change: A Replication in New Mexico," *Educational Administration Quarterly*, vol. 9 (Autumn 1973), pp. 48-65. In turn, this article was critiqued carefully in Frank W. Lutz, "The Role of Explanatory Models in Theory Building: In Response to LeDoux-Burlingame," *Educational Administration Quarterly*, vol. 11 (Winter 1975), pp. 72-78.

School Board Response and Incumbent Defeat

William L. Garberina, Sr.

Introduction

The purpose of this chapter is to investigate the relationship between the demand-response behavior of school boards and incumbent school board member defeat. *Demand* is defined as public demand as operationalized by social, economic, and political indicators used in the former studies. (These indicators are listed in appendixes 6A and 6B.) *Response* is defined as school board response to public demand as operationalized by the school tax levy. (These indicators are also listed in appendix 6C.)

The road to incumbent school board member defeat and the subsequent involuntary turnover of the superintendent have been detailed by Iannaccone and Lutz.[1] As the characteristics of school districts change, a gap may develop between the values and attitudes of the school board and the community. As the population shifts through increases or mobility, a shift occurs in the community's socioeconomic class. Meanwhile, the school board may remain relatively unchanged in membership and values. It becomes progressively segregated from the school district. As the gap widens, the community will attempt to prevent this segregation, and if it fails to do so, school board member defeat will generally follow.

In an attempt to operationalize the model, Kirkendall developed eleven social and economic indicators and eight political indicators of community conditions, based on the model, that would predict the road to incumbent school board member defeat.[2] He was able to discriminate between those districts which had experienced incumbent school board member defeat and those in which it did not occur.

LeDoux and Burlingame reported efforts to replicate the California study.[3] Using data collected from school districts in New Mexico, these authors found that the 19 socioeconomic and political indicators did not predict incumbent school board member defeat as well as the Kirkendall study. This occurrence was attributed to a downward trend in the socioeconomic and political indicators in the New Mexico study. The authors attribute this fact to a weakness in the model, stating that the model accounts for only indicators that are showing an upward trend.

Theoretical Framework

Lutz states that decreases in socioeconomic indicators in the community may not predict either incumbent defeat or superintendent turnover as effectively because politicians are generally quicker to reduce taxes in times of economic decline than they are to raise taxes in times of economic rise.[4] It appeared that this factor could account for the less effective predictability rate of the New Mexico study. In neither the California nor the New Mexico study were the school boards' responses to the socioeconomic and political trends in the communities considered. The school boards' responses to these trends, as indicated by the fluctuation or lack of fluctuation of the tax rate, should identify the *gap* and thus the predictability of incumbent school board member defeat in school districts showing a downward trend in socioeconomic and political indicators.

When the socioeconomic and political indicators in a school district are increasing and the demand-response indicator of the school board is increasing, an educational gap will not exist between the community and the school board. This would also be true of downward trends. However, when the socioeconomic and political trends in a community are in disagreement with the response indicator (tax rate set by the school board), an educational gap in a school district is more likely to exist. Incumbent school board member defeat is more probable in school districts that have indicator disagreement than in school districts with indicator agreement.

In examining the relationship between the demand-response indicator of school boards and incumbent school board member defeat, six hypotheses were developed in this study:

H_1 There will be no significant relationship between the social, economic, and political indicators of community conditions and school districts that experience or do not experience incumbent school board member defeat.

H_2 There will be no significant relationship between the social, economic, and political indicators of community conditions showing an upward trend and school districts that experience or do not experience incumbent school board member defeat.

H_3 There will be no significant relationship between the social, economic, and political indicators of community conditions showing a downward trend and school districts that experience or do not experience incumbent school board member defeat.

These first three hypotheses were tested using the same socioeconomic and political indicators as the Kirkendall and LeDoux and Burlingame studies. The final three hypotheses used the same indicators, but also included the response factor to determine if the prediction of incumbent defeat could be improved. They are as follows:

H_4 There will be no significant relationship between the social, economic, and political indicators of community conditions and the demand-response of school boards to these conditions and school districts that experience or do not experience incumbent school board member defeat.

H_5 There will be no significant relationship between the social, economic, and political indicators of community conditions showing an upward trend and the demand-response of school boards to these conditions and school districts that experience or do not experience incumbent school board member defeat.

H_6 There will be no significant relationship between the social, economic, and political indicators of community conditions showing a downward trend and the demand-response to school boards to these conditions and school districts that experience or do not experience incumbent school board member defeat.

The Sample, Data Collection, and Method

The sample of 77 school districts used in this study was selected from the 351 school systems in Massachusetts. Only those school districts were used that offered a unified K to 12 program or 1 to 12 program and that did not share facilities with other school systems. The final sample of 77 school systems represents rural, suburban, and urban areas, growing and declining communities, and different socioeconomic settings.

The sample school districts were grouped into four categories: incumbent defeat, no incumbent defeat school districts, and districts experiencing growth or decline in the socioeconomic and political indicators. A school district was considered in a downward trend if at least two of the general indicators were declining. Table 6-1 presents the categorization of the school districts.

The specific indicators used in this study are based on the 19 variables used by Kirkendall in California and LeDoux in New Mexico[5] (appendix 6C). This study utilized socioeconomic indicators in the 10-year span prior to the 1973

Table 6-1
Number of School Districts Experiencing Incumbent-No Incumbent Defeat by Socioeconomic and Political Indicator Trend

| | | Indicator Trend | |
| | Combined | Upward | Downward |
Incumbent Defeat	(Group 1)	(Group 2)	(Group 3)
Yes	21	19	2
No	56	42	14
Total	77	61	16

school board elections. The increases or decreases in political conditions in the sample school districts were determined by examining the school board elections of 1971 and 1972. Each year one-third of all school board seats expire in Massachusetts, regardless of the size of the school board. Hence, the 1971 and 1972 elections represented an opportunity for the community to elect a new majority to the school board.

The specific indicators used to measure changes in the response of school boards to community conditions (appendix 6C) represented all the possible time spans, given a 10-year period, that can be included with 1972 as the year of termination. The use of these eight indicators allowed for a determination of the amount of change in the tax rate which a community will bear before the defeat of a school board incumbent will occur.

A multiple regression analysis was used to analyze the relationship among the selected variables. The statistics were successively recomputed, based on the exclusion of the least significant independent variable, one at a time.

Data Analyses

H_1: Group 1 School Districts—Socioeconomic and Political Indicators

Variables 4 and 6 were eliminated prior to the analysis. They did not contribute significantly to the zero-order correlation matrix. The multiple regression analysis was performed using 17 variables. H_1 was not rejected using 17 variables. Following the pattern of the previous studies, the ten strongest indicators were then selected for analysis. Although the ten indicators (1, 2, 3, 8, 9, 10, 12, 13, 17, and 19)—see appendixes 6A and 6B) accounted for less explained variance than the 17, 33.7 percent to 31.1 percent, these ten produced an R of .557, significant at the .01 level.

A successive reduction, one at a time, of the ten through six strongest indicators (3, 8, 9, 10, 12, 13) was attempted. Significant results at the .01 level were obtained for all groups of the nine through six strongest socioeconomic-political indicators.

Although significant results were obtained after the initial analysis of 17 was reduced to the ten strongest, these results should be interpreted cautiously. An explained variance of .311, using ten indicators provides for the inclusion of other variables which may improve the prediction of defeat of incumbent school board members. Also, the inclusion of school districts showing both an upward and a downward trend in the socioeconomic and political indicators affected the homogeneity of variance; the result was a smaller fraction of explained variance using the combined group 1 school districts than occurred when that combined sample was split into two groups—those moving upward in indicators and those moving downward.

H₄: Group 1 (Combined) School Districts—Socioeconomic, Political, Demand-Response Indicators

This test added the demand-response indicators to the original socioeconomic and political indicators. Since the 17 variables used in H_1 were not significantly related to incumbent defeat, only the ten strongest indicators, previously determined, were used to test this hypothesis.

The addition of the eight demand-response indicators failed to contribute significantly to the explained variance when added to the ten strongest socioeconomic and political indicators in group 1 (combined) school districts. The demand-response indicators did not make a significant contribution to the prediction of incumbent defeat until six of the eight response indicators had been eliminated. The addition of two tax response variables (26, 27) to the ten socioeconomic political variables allows one to account for an additional 4.4 percent of the variance in incumbent defeat. These ten strongest socioeconomic-political variables plus two demand-response indicators produced an R of .576, accounting for 33.2 percent of the variance in incumbent defeat. This is only a slight improvement over the ten socioeconomic-political variables used alone.

H₂: Group 2 (Upward) School Districts— Socioeconomic-Political Indicators

Again variables 4 and 6 were immediately eliminated as not contributing to the explained variance. The multiple regression analysis using 17 variables produced an F ratio of 1.76 which was not significant at the .01 level. The multiple R of .6332 accounted for 40.1 percent of the explained variance.

Although the null hypothesis could not reject using 17 variables, the explained variance of 40.1 percent for group 2 school districts showed an increase over the explained variance of 33.7 percent for group 1 school districts.

A progressive elimination of the one indicator which made the least contribution to the multiple regression analysis was made, starting with the ten strongest indicators and reducing them to six. These subsequent tests produced significant results in all tests at the .01 level. Using the ten strongest socioeconomic-political variables, in group 2 (upward) districts, a multiple R of .598 was obtained, accounting for 35.8 percent of the variance in incumbent defeat in upward districts.

In group 1 and group 2 school districts, variables concerned with assessed valuation were eliminated early in the multiple regression analysis. This trend indicates the lack of influence of changes in assessed valuation in Massachusetts on school board elections. However, when these changes adversely affect the per pupil cost, and thus educational programs for pupils, incumbent school board members are defeated.

The number of voters that turn out for school board elections in Massachusetts is a better predictor of incumbent defeat than the number of candidates challenging incumbents for their positions. Although other political indicators appear in the ten strongest indicators, they are eliminated in both group 1 and group 2 school districts as the variables decrease. Indicators 17 and 19 appear among the ten strongest variables in both group 1 and group 2 school districts. *The trend toward incumbent defeat, in Massachusetts, therefore, can be viewed by school board members by observing the defeat of any of their colleagues in the election year that precedes the expiration of their term by two years.*

H_5: Group 2 (Upward) School Districts—Socioeconomic, Political, and Demand-Response Indicators

The ten strongest socioeconomic-political indicators were used with the eight response indicators. The F ratio of 2.21 was not significant at the .01 level. The multiple R of .6974 accounted for 48.6 percent of the explained variance. The inclusion of the eight demand-response indicators to the ten strongest socioeconomic indicators did not significantly improve the amount of variance accounted for in incumbent defeat, in group 2 school districts. The inclusion of the eight response indicators, however, increased the amount of explained variance by 12.8 percent over the 35.8 percent obtained by the ten strongest socioeconomic and political indicators alone.

A progressive elimination of the one indicator which made the least contribution to the multiple regression analysis was made, starting with the combined 18 indicators and reducing them to ten. The response indicators produced a significant multiple R in group 2 school districts after the elimination of variables 24 and 25. Although accounting for larger portions of the explained variance in group 2 school districts, the response indicators continued to be eliminated with the exception of variable 23 (percent of change in the tax rate over the last 7 years).

H_3: Group 3 (Downward) School Districts—Socioeconomic and Political Indicators

Since all available group 3 school districts numbered 16, there were more predictors when all 19 socioeconomic-political variables were used than there were school districts. Hence, there were not enough observations with respect to the number of variables in this problem. Since all possible districts with group 3 were already in the sample, sample size could not be increased. Thus other methods of investigating the problem were sought.

H_6: Group 3 (Downward) School Districts—Socioeconomic, Political, and Demand-Response Indicators

Since the number of observations was smaller than the number of variables for this problem, the hypothesis was tested by using the three strongest social, economic, and political indicators (1, 2, and 8) and the eight demand-response indicators. The combination of the three strongest socioeconomic and political indicators and the eight response indicators produced an *F* ratio of 2.37 that was not significant at the .01 level. A multiple *R* of .9313 accounted for 86.7 percent of the explained variance. The large amount of explained variance without a significant *F* ratio indicates the need for a larger *n*. Due to the small number of observations and the large amount of explained variance, the possibility of Type II error could account for this lack of significant results. Games and Klare[6] explain that a Type II error occurs if the null hypothesis is false; yet we obtain a statistic that falls in the probable region and hence retain the null hypothesis. The risk of a Type II error can be reduced while holding the level of significance constant by increasing the number of observations. All available information of incumbent defeat in Massachusetts in group 3 (downward) school districts, however, amounted to 16 observations. The number of observations could not be increased to reduce the risk of a Type II error.

A progressive elimination of the one indicator which made the least contribution to the multiple regression analysis, as indicated by its partial coefficient, was made, starting with the eleven strongest combined indicators and reducing them to three. The two strongest response indicators (20 and 21) and the one strongest socioeconomic indicator (8) produced a multiple *R* of .8114, accounting for 65.8 percent of the explained variance. An *F* ratio of 7.71 was significant at the .01 level. It is important to note that after the elimination of variables 22 and 27, the demand-response indicators and the socioeconomic and political indicators produced significant results at the .01 level.

Table 6-2 summarizes the results of the multiple regression analysis of the progressive elimination of the eleven through three strongest indicators with regard to incumbent defeat in group 3 school districts. The data tend to confirm the possibility that a Type II error has occurred regarding H_6. Games and Klare[7] state that a reduction in the required level of significance reduces the risk of a Type II error when the number of observations remains constant. The number of observations was 16 for H_6. Originally the risk of a Type I error was set at the .01 level. Results significant at the .05 level after the elimination of two variables indicate that an increase in the observations for H_6 might produce significant results at the .05 level for the first three tests.

The above analyses suggest that the response indicator is an important variable in predicting incumbent school board member defeat in school districts

Table 6-2
Results of Statistical Analysis for H_6 Using Eleven to Three Strongest Socioeconomic, Political, and Demand-Response Indicators in Group 3 (Downward) School Districts

Number of Variables[a]	df	R	Explained Variance	F Ratio	Significance
3 + 8	11,4	0.9313	0.867	2.37	n.s.
3 + 7	10,5	0.9289	0.863	3.14	n.s.
3 + 6	9,6	0.9270	0.859	4.07	n.s.
3 + 5	8,7	0.9167	0.840	4.60	.05
2 + 5	7,8	0.9056	0.820	5.20	.05
1 + 5	6,9	0.8684	0.754	4.59	.05
1 + 4	5,10	0.8393	0.704	4.67	.05
1 + 3	4,11	0.8205	0.673	5.66	.05
1 + 2	3,12	0.8114	0.658	7.71	.01
$n = 16$					

[a]Numbers in left-hand column represent total number of socioeconomic and political indicators for each test. Numbers in right-hand column represent total number of demand-response indicators for each test.

showing a *downward* trend in the socioeconomic and political indicators. This conclusion is based on the following:

1. The large amount of variance (86.7 percent) explained by the eleven strongest indicators, including response variables
2. The significant result produced at the .01 level by the three strongest indicators
3. The significant results produced by the eight through four strongest indicators at the .05 level

Therefore, the relatively lower predictability of the Iannaccone-Lutz model found by LeDoux in incumbent school board member defeat in school districts showing a downward trend can be explained, in part, by the inclusion of the school board tax response indicator into the operational model.

The same combined eleven indicators were applied to group 1 (combined) school districts with regard to incumbent defeat. An *F* ratio of 0.760 was not significant at the .01 level. A multiple *R* of .337 accounted for 11.4 percent of the explained variance. A progressive elimination of each indicator that contributed least to the multiple regression, as indicated by the partial coefficient, failed to produce any significant results. The amount of explained variance, ranging from 11.4 percent to 9.5 percent, is the result of a lack of homogeneity of variance when group 2 and group 3 school districts are combined. The results tend to confirm the findings of H_4, as previously reported. Although significant results at the .01 level were found for the last three tests of the hypothesis, the inclusion of the response indicators reduced the amount of explained variance. Therefore, the importance of the response indicator as a predictor of incumbent defeat, without accounting for the trend of the socioeconomic and political indicators, seems counterproductive.

Ancillary Findings

The multiple correlations of the three strongest socioeconomic-political indicators plus the eight demand-response indicators with incumbent defeat for group 2 (upward) and group 3 (downward) school districts were examined to determine if there was a significant difference between them. A Fisher Z transformation produced a Z score of .50 for the group 2 school districts and a Z score of 1.66 for the group 3 school districts. The difference between the Z scores produced a t of 3.90 which was significant at the .005 level. There was a significant difference between the prediction of incumbent defeat in group 3 (downward) school districts as compared to group 2 (upward) school districts, using the response indicators. Table 6-3 summarizes the results of the statistical analysis.

Conclusions

The following conclusions are offered with cautions previously cited.[8]

1. The tax response of school boards in declining communities has a significant effect on school board elections.
2. The response indicator is an important variable in predicting incumbent school board member defeat in declining communities.
3. H_6, as stated, is worthy of further consideration when a larger number of observations are available.

Table 6-3
Statistical Analysis between Group 2 and Group 3 School Districts

Districts	n	R	Explained Variance	F Ratio	Z Score
Group 2	61	.468	.219	0.102	0.50[a]
Group 3	16	.931	.867	2.37	1.66[a]

[a]Difference significant at the .005 level.

4. The amount of explained variance of 86.7 percent indicates that the response indicator, used to predict incumbent defeat in declining communities, assists in explaining the theoretical gap found by LeDoux and Burlingame in the Kirkendall model.

5. School board members running for reelection in declining communities should consider the tax response of the school board to community conditions if they wish to be reelected.

6. The response factor is a significant variable in predicting incumbent school board member defeat. This is especially true in declining communities.

The extension of the Kirkendall operational model in this study to include the response of the school board to community conditions shows a direct relationship between incumbent defeat and the demand-response of school boards. The superintendent's tenure is affected by the composition of the school board. A study examining the effects of the demand-response indicators on involuntary superintendent turnover might help determine the reason that some superintendents survive incumbent defeat while others do not. If the response indicators have the same trend as the demand socioeconomic and political indicators, then a gap does not exist between the school board policy and community educational values. If an incumbent is defeated under these conditions, the defeat could be a result of noneducational issues. It could be that the superintendent would not experience involuntary turnover under such conditions.

The studies of incumbent defeat in California, New Mexico, and Massachusetts have been post hoc analyses of this phenomenon. An examination of the ability of the operational indicators to predict incumbent defeat prior to school board elections would be useful. If the results of this type of study were unsuccessful, future researchers could modify the operational model to include other indicators of community conditions that would be better predictors of incumbent defeat. If the results of this type of study were successful, the operational indicators would provide school boards with a means to develop educational policy that meets the needs of the communities they serve. With the minimization of the potential for incumbent defeat, school boards may be less fearful of open debate over educational policy. When school boards are not fearful of open debate, educational policy can be developed that is consistent with the changing needs of the environment that they serve.

Notes

1. For a complete description of the model, see Laurence Iannaccone and Frank W. Lutz, *Politics, Power and Policy: The Governance of Local School Districts* (Columbus, Ohio: Charles E. Merrill Publishing Company, 1970), pp. 85-88.

2. Richard S. Kirkendall, "Discriminating Social, Economic and Political Characteristics of Changing versus Stable Policy-Making Systems in School Districts," unpublished Ph.D. dissertation, Claremont Graduate School, 1966.

3. Eugene P. LeDoux and Martin Burlingame, "The Iannaccone-Lutz Model of School Board Change: A Replication in New Mexico," *Educational Administration Quarterly*, vol. 9, no. 3 (Autumn 1973), pp. 48-65.

4. Frank W. Lutz, "The Role of Explanatory Models in Theory Building: In Response to LeDoux-Burlingame," *Educational Administration Quarterly*, vol. 11, no. 1 (Winter 1975), p. 75.

5. Eugene P. LeDoux, "Outmigration: Its Relation to Social, Political and Economic Conditions and to the Governing of Local School Districts in New Mexico," unpublished Ph.D. dissertation, University of New Mexico, 1971.

6. Paul A. Games and George R. Klare, *Elementary Statistics: Data Analysis for the Behavioral Sciences* (New York: McGraw-Hill Book Company, 1967), pp. 279-282.

7. Ibid., p. 282.

8. William L. Garberina, Sr., "Public Demand, School Board Response and Incumbent Defeat: An Examination of the Governance of Local School Districts in Massachusetts," unpublished Ph.D. dissertation, Pennsylvania State University, 1975.

Appendix 6A
Specific Socioeconomic
Indicators[a]

1. Percent change in net average membership over the 3-year period: (1956-1957 to 1959-1960), [1966-1967 to 1969-1970], 1968-1969 to 1971-1972.
2. Percent change in net average membership over the 3-year period: (1954-1955 to 1957-1958), [1965-1966 to 1967-1968], 1966-1967 to 1969-1970.
3. Percent change in net average membership over the 6-year period: (1951-1952 to 1959-1960), [1961-1962 to 1967-1968], 1964-1965 to 1969-1970.
4. Percent change in net average membership over the 8-year period: (1951-1952 to 1959-1960), [1961-1962 to 1969-1970], 1963-1964 to 1971-1972.
5. Percent change in assessed valuation over the 3-year period: (1951-1952 to 1954-1955), [1961-1962 to 1964-1965], 1963-1964 to 1966-1967.
6. Percent change in assessed valuation over the 6-year period: (1951-1952 to 1957-1958), [1961-1962 to 1967-1968], 1963-1964 to 1969-1970.
7. Percent change in assessed valuation over the 8-year period: (1951-1952 to 1959-1960), [1961-1962 to 1969-1970], 1963-1964 to 1971-1972.
8. Change in assessed valuation per net average membership over the 3-year period: (1956-1957 to 1959-1960), [1966-1967 to 1969-1970], 1968-1969 to 1971-1972.
9. Change in assessed valuation per net average membership over the 3-year period: (1954-1955 to 1957-1958), [1964-1965 to 1967-1968], 1966-1967 to 1969-1970.
10. Percent change in assessed valuation per net average membership over the 3-year period: (1956-1957 to 1959-1960), [1966-1967 to 1969-1970], 1968-1969 to 1971-1972.
11. Percent change in assessed valuation per net average membership over the 3-year period: (1955-1956 to 1958-1959), [1966-1967 to 1968-1969], 1967-1968 to 1970-1971.

[a]The years used in the California study appear in parentheses; the years used in the New Mexico study appear in brackets; the years used in the Massachusetts study appear last, without parentheses or brackets.

Appendix 6B
Specific Political
Indicators[a]

12. Ratio of votes against incumbents to total votes cast in the (1959), [1969], 1972, school board elections.
13. Ratio of votes against incumbents to total votes cast in the (1958), [1967], 1971, school board elections.
14. Ratio of candidates to positions in the (1961), [1971], 1972, school board elections.
15. Ratio of candidates to positions in the (1959), [1969], 1971, school board elections.
16. Incumbent index for the (ratio of candidates to positions in the 1958 school board elections), [ratio of candidates to positions in the 1967 school board elections], 1972 school board elections.
17. Incumbent index for the (1958), [1967], 1971, school board elections.
18. Board election index for the (1959), [1969], 1972, school board elections.
19. Board election index for the (1958), [1967], 1971, school board elections.

---

[a]The years used in the California study appear in parentheses; the years used in the New Mexico study appear in brackets; the years used in the Massachusetts study appear last, without parentheses or brackets.

Appendix 6C
Demand-Response Tax
Indicators Used Only in
the Massachusetts Study

20. Percent change in the tax rate over the 10-year period 1962-1963 to 1971-1972.
21. Percent change in the tax rate over the 9-year period 1963-1964 to 1971-1972.
22. Percent change in the tax rate over the 8-year period 1964-1965 to 1971-1972.
23. Percent change in the tax rate over the 7-year period 1965-1966 to 1971-1972.
24. Percent change in the tax rate over the 6-year period 1966-1967 to 1971-1972.
25. Percent change in the tax rate over the 5-year period 1967-1968 to 1971-1972.
26. Percent change in the tax rate over the 4-year period 1968-1969 to 1971-1972.
27. Percent change in the tax rate over the 3-year period 1969-1970 to 1971-1972.

7

Measurement and Methodological Issues Related to Research on Incumbent Defeat and Superintendent Turnover

Douglas E. Mitchell

Introduction

The purpose of this chapter is to examine the major methodological issues which arise from an assessment of one strand of school governance research—the one historically associated with the names of Laurence Iannaccone and Frank W. Lutz[1] and most deeply concerned with the importance of electoral defeats for incumbent school board members and the turnover of school superintendents. Initially, the focus will be on the divergence in methodology and findings between this line of research and other major strands of inquiry. Also of concern, however, are some methodological problems which need to be resolved in order to strengthen this line of research and fully test the significance of the incumbent defeat-superintendent turnover processes.

Broadly speaking, methodological issues related to incumbent defeat—superintendent turnover research arise at three distinct levels: (1) the theoretical conception and design level, where different perspectives lead researchers to seek different sorts of data for analysis; (2) the variable measurement level, where different theories and research interests interact with practical field problems to control the availability and reliability of indicators being used in testing research hypotheses; and (3) the data analysis level, where the choice of procedures for testing hypotheses may or may not be appropriate to the conclusions which are drawn. The remainder of this chapter is divided into three sections dealing with each of these three methodological levels.

Theoretical Design Issues

At the most general level, methodological evaluation of any line of research is concerned with relationships between the design of the research and the underlying theory on which that design is based. Whether the research is primarily exploratory and aimed at theory building or confirmatory and aimed at theory testing, it is important to examine how adequately the theoretical hypotheses utilized by the researchers account for their data. At this level, research examining the role of incumbent defeat (ID) and superintendent turnover (STO) in local school district governance presents two basic problems.

73

First, the theory of democratic control which has characterized the research following the Iannaccone-Lutz model is unique in the study of school governance. This unique theory has not been adequately appreciated by most researchers who have concluded, with Zeigler and Jennings,[2] that democratic control of school policy is more illusion than reality. This failure to appreciate the theoretical uniqueness of the ID-STO research strand not only has led to the development of research designs which are difficult to compare but also has permitted many researchers to overlook or ignore this potentially vital mechanism of citizen influence on school policy formation.

A second theoretical design-level problem is more internal to the cluster of research efforts devoted to the study of incumbent defeat and superintendent turnover. The central hypothesis of this research asserts that incumbent defeat and superintendent turnover represent the *episodic* realignment of the school board and school management with the values and ideological norms (i.e., the culture) of school district populations which have changed in their orientations toward school policy more quickly than has the governing board. This conception that change is episodic has not been defined clearly enough in research thus far reported, which leads to some important problems of interpretation. The nature of the hypothesized policy change episodes needs to be carefully examined in order to determine when research designs have been adequately constructed and executed.

Let us take up each of these problems in order.

A Dissatisfaction Theory of Democratic Control

The single most important feature of research on incumbent defeat (ID) and superintendent turnover (STO) has been the unique theory of democratic control which it represents. Most efforts to study political processes and political behavior in America have been motivated by a desire to determine whether and/or in what ways democratic theory is being realized or violated in the organizational structures and political processes of our society. It is important to recognize that this explicit attempt to apply democratic values to school district operations provides the major theoretical hypotheses which these research efforts have been seeking to test. Of course, the fact that most researchers begin by asking some form of the question, "Are the school districts democratic" does not mean that they agree about the answer to their question, or even about the meaning of the term *democratic*. While most researchers have been loudly proclaiming that schools are definitely *not* controlled democratically, research following the Iannaccone-Lutz[3] model has continued to insist that there is a firm, though somewhat surprising, "yes" answer to the question of whether democracy is alive and well in local school governance.

From a methodological perspective, the problem becomes a matter of how to decide whether democratic control really exists. Three essentially different versions of democratic control are found in the literature on school governance. These different versions provide different concepts of democracy and different tests for its reality. The first is illustrated by the essays found in Fredrick Wirt's book *The Polity of the School.*[4] The scholars whose works are found in this book tend to embrace what might be called a *responsiveness* theory of democracy. The principle criterion for the presence or absence of democratic control, from the viewpoint of this theory, is whether or not there is a measurable shift in school policy which results when identifiable demands for action are expressed by citizens. A second theory of democratic theory is indebted to the work of David Minar[5] and is articulated by Zeigler and Jennings in *Governing American Schools.*[6] This book tests school politics with what could be called a *competition* theory of democracy. Zeigler and Jennings conceive of a truly democratic process of governance as one characterized by continuous, informed competition between individuals and groups who have specific interests in specific policy outcomes. Researchers embracing this model believe that democratic processes will, of necessity, involve electoral conflict and competition which lead to changing patterns of success and failure for political candidates with divergent policy commitments. Iannaccone and Lutz offer the third theory of democratic control. As presented in their book *Politics, Power and Policy: The Governing of Local Schools,*[7] these authors hold what might be called a *dissatisfaction* theory of democracy. According to this model, democracy is expressed through the periodic readjustment of government policy in response to deeply felt and politically expressed dissatisfaction of the school district citizenry with the continuing and fairly stable school policy formulated by the school board and superintendent.

Each of these three views of democratic control finds a different use for data related to school district elections and school board candidates. The responsiveness theorists tend to look at the electoral process as a *communications link* through which demands and supports for the school professionals and school boards are transmitted. In this model, elections are generally not thought to be, in themselves, mechanisms of either control or response. Democratic responsiveness is, instead, measured by examining the school system's direct actions on policy matters and educational programs. Thus these theorists use electoral data to determine whether "demand" or "support" is present in the system, but not to determine whether a policy shift or response is actually in progress.

From the perspective of the competition theorists, two pieces of evidence seem to be conclusive in demonstrating that school elections contain weak or nonexistent democratic control mechanisms. First, statistically speaking, school elections typically contain only the most meager competition for seats on the governing board. And second, what competition does exist tends to be very poorly informed, which makes it hard to believe that it springs from policy rather than mere personal considerations. Furthermore, research based on this theory finds that school boards frequently do not control policy decisions. Instead, the policy process seems to be dominated by the school superintendent. This seems to lead naturally to the conclusion that what little democratic control citizens do exercise in the election of school board members is quickly lost in the interaction between the board and the superintendent.

From the perspective of the dissatisfaction theory, however, political competition and issue responsiveness are insufficient measures of democratic control. The dissatisfaction theory finds issue-based responsiveness to be an inadequate test because most school policy matters never reach enough clarity to become salient issues and therefore cannot be properly analyzed in terms of responsiveness to specific demands. That is, the dissatisfaction theory is based on a belief that school district citizens have essentially diffuse expectations about the quality and nature of the schooling which should be provided by the board and superintendent, and that they do not have either the interest or the detailed information needed to make specific policy demands. Citizens probably know when policy is not right, but they do not generally have very precise views on how it should be different. The dissatisfaction theory also finds that electoral competition and conflict are not adequate measures of democratic control either. As the Iannaccone-Lutz model sees it, vigorous political conflict and frequent policy change are certainly not indicators of democratic control for the large numbers of citizens who are seeking stability and quiescence in school policy matters. For this model, citizens faced with undesired policy change would be governed just as undemocratically as are those who are faced with undesired stability and resistance to change.

The dissatisfaction model hypothesizes that ideological or value commitments of district citizens are the essential ingredients in any democratic control process. The ID-STO hypothesis which is central to this theory has been developed as a broad indicator of the flow of changed ideological and value commitments from the citizens to the school management system. Because of the absence of effective ideological measurements, the ID-STO process has been conceptualized as a relatively crude but substantial indicator that district citizens are utilizing school board elections to present a "change" or a "no-change" mandate to the school policy makers. By studying the change/no-change policy mandates reflected in the occurrences of incumbent defeat and superintendent turnover, Iannaccone and Lutz concluded that school districts *are* democratically controlled, at least to the extent that change mandates do arise within the school district citizenry and that these change mandates are passed to the board through the electoral process and finally come to fruition in the policy changes made as a result of a turnover in the district's chief executive officer.

In addition to having this unique operational definition of democratic control, dissatisfaction theorists have utilized a unique approach to research design. While other researchers have sought large-scale random samples of *typical* school elections for analysis, researchers following this theory have single-mindedly insisted upon studying the correlates of the two key events: incumbent defeat and superintendent turnover. It is important to recognize that under certain, not implausible, conditions research utilizing designs inspired by responsiveness and competition theories of democracy would completely miss the operation of democratic policy control working through the ID and STO vehicles identified as pivotal by the dissatisfaction theorists. To be specific, there are four conditions which, if true, would make it completely impossible for even very large-scale random samples to detect the presence of effective and powerful democratic controls operating through episodic surges of dissatisfaction among district voters. First, if it is true that the desire of citizens to change school policy is not always intense and is not randomly distributed across districts or among citizens, but rather arises in response to specific changed circumstances within the district, then the focusing of a critical mass of dissatisfaction on a particular school governance system would be difficult to locate within a large random sample of citizens.

Second, if it is also true that when voters take the relatively unusual step of defeating an incumbent school board member at the polls, this is taken by other board members as solid evidence of a desire for policy change and this causes them to turn to the successful insurgent board member for guidance and direction on district policy,[a] *then* large-scale samples of school board members would miss the vital leadership role played by these insurgents.

Third, if it is also true that there are fairly short periods within the life history of the school district when policy changes are made in a fairly rapid and dramatic way and longer periods when policy is stable and unchanging (in accordance with the wishes of most citizens), then large-scale random sample studies would simply show that most districts were not undergoing any policy shift.

Finally, if it takes time for citizen dissatisfactions to become sufficiently well focused to affect the outcome of an election, and still more time for the change mandate generated by an incumbent defeat to effectively alter school policy in the desired direction, then large-scale, short-time-span studies would make it appear as though policy changes were occurring in districts where they were not desired and not occurring in those where they were desired. Analysis of data gathered under these four conditions would appear to indicate (exactly as described by Zeigler and Jennings) that informed political competition is generally low and that responsiveness to specific citizen policy demands is weak or nonexistent. Under the specific conditions, only a diachronic data gathering and analysis procedure which specifically tests for the contingency of policy change upon the crucial political events of ID and STO will lead to the conclusion that electoral democracy in the school districts works by providing

[a]This process is well documented in the Robertsdale case examined by Iannaccone and Lutz; see especially chapter 7.

the necessary mechanisms to both stabilize citizen satisfactions and transform citizen dissatisfactions into effective mandates for school policy and program change.

Episodic Instability and ID-STO Research

Certainly the most important hypothesis advanced by the dissatisfaction theory of democratic control is that school policy change tends to be *episodic* (that is, abrupt and infrequent) rather than gradual or continuous. This idea that school policy is characterized by longish periods of quiescence and stability, interrupted by fairly brief episodes of abrupt change, creates some important problems for research design. The first problem is to determine whether any short periods within the life history of a school district actually involve the hypothesized dramatic changes in policy. Richard Carlson[8] and J.A. Reynolds[9] have provided the apparently definitive answer to this question by showing that new superintendents, particularly if they come from outside the school district at the time of their appointment, make many more policy, personnel, and programmatic changes in their first two years in office than at any other time. These works have thus become the basis for arguing that change episodes can be clearly identified by means of the appointment of new superintendents, at least if they are outsiders.

This recognition that episodic change is connected to executive succession has led researchers holding the dissatisfaction theory of democracy to search for the causes of STO and to identify the electoral defeat of incumbent school board members as an effective predictor of turnover and therefore of episodic policy change. Extended field study of the Robertsdale school district by Iannaccone and Lutz,[10] followed by the Walden[11] and Freeborn[12] doctoral dissertations under Iannaccone's direction, has generally been taken as conclusively establishing the connection between ID and STO. More recent work, however, has begun to raise some questions with Walden's and Freeborn's findings. For example, while Moen's work on partisan elections in Pennsylvania has supported the applicability of the ID-STO hypothesis to the *involuntary* turnover of superintendents in that state, his data do not appear to support a relationship between ID and the *total* rate of STO (voluntary and involuntary) and diverge from Walden's and Freeborn's findings in this respect.[b] Moreover, in a 1975 study, Eblen claims that his data directly challenge the ID-STO

---

[b]Freeborn examined the problem of involuntary turnover in the Walden/Freeborn data. His results on this point concur with Moen's findings. However, while confining attention exclusively to *involuntary* turnovers may reduce inconsistency in the findings, the absolute number of involuntary turnover among superintendents is rather small. Therefore, to consider only involuntary superintendent turnover as the major mechanism of democratic control makes the instances of democratic action too rare to be considered a serious defense of democracy in the schools.

hypothesis, since he was unable to confirm the existence of a statistically significant relationship between ID and STO over an 18-year period in 37 northern Illinois school districts. Although his study is seriously flawed in its measurement and data analysis phases (in ways to be discussed in third and fourth sections), it does prompt a careful review of just what the dissatisfaction theory should lead us to expect about a relationship between the occurrence of ID and STO within local school districts.

There are two points to keep in mind when considering how dissatisfaction theory expects ID and STO to fit into the process of school governance. The first point is that research based on this theory is shaped by the belief that the ultimate theoretical variables are *citizen dissatisfaction* and *policy change*. ID and STO are only hypothesized to be *operational indicators* which record the *flow* of dissatisfaction from the district citizenry to the school management system. As with all operational indicators, dissatisfaction theory makes no claim either that dissatisfactions are transmitted *only* through ID and STO or that the rates of ID and STO depend *exclusively* on the dissatisfaction of district voters. Take, for example, an obvious case: even the most beloved of superintendents may die, retire, or be hired away to a higher-paying district, giving rise to a STO which does not indicate the slightest dissatisfaction with existing district policies.[c] It is equally possible that some incumbent board members will be defeated because they have violated community norms in some way completely unrelated to school policy making, such as getting divorced or committing a crime. This type of ID would not, of course, be indicative of dissatisfaction with present policy, and STO would not be expected to occur more frequently under these circumstances than if an incumbent had retired without seeking reelection.

In the design and execution of research, there are two possible approaches to this expectation that factors other than dissatisfaction will affect the rates of ID and STO. The typical approach has been to hope that these extraneous sources of ID and STO are randomly distributed and cause only a relatively small proportion of all board and superintendent changes. When this hope is fulfilled, a sufficiently large sample will always reveal that the episodes of dissatisfaction connect ID with STO at a statistically significant frequency. If this hope is not well founded, however, another approach must be taken. The second approach requires that other important sources of the variance in the rate of ID and STO be identified and measured, and that appropriate statistical data analysis techniques be used so as to remove the effects of these theoretically unimportant but still substantial sources of variability in the key indicator variables. Since the available data have produced mixed findings regarding the connection between ID and STO, the second approach will be essential in future research on

---

[c]This is not to suggest, however, that only nonpolitical motives account for voluntary superintendent turnover. It seems quite reasonable to assume that many superintendents move voluntarily when they recognize that there is resistence to their policies or a desire for new leadership within the district.

this topic. Specific suggestions for the implementation of this approach will be discussed further in the third and fourth sections.

In addition to the need for carefully controlling the effects of variables not related to citizen dissatisfaction on the rates of ID and STO, it is also important to recognize the importance of *time* as a basic conceptual variable in the dissatisfaction theory of school governance. Dissatisfaction theory expects that there will be a time lag at each step in the democratic governance process as control moves from citizen dissatisfaction to incumbent defeat, from defeat to superintendent turnover, and from turnover to significant policy change. That is, at least a few months and perhaps several years will be required for the democratic control process to effect a realignment of the school management with district citizens' desires. Just as episodes of political upheaval and instability are expected to extend over some period of time, dissatisfaction theorists hypothesize that the periods of quiescence and stability between the episodic change periods will also extend over significant periods. Research thus far reported sheds a little light on the length of time between critical events within the episodes of upheaval and change. Based on Carlson's work, significant policy change appears to take up to 2 years following a STO. Walden,[13] Moen,[14] and Eblen[15] all thought that there might be 3 or perhaps 4 years between ID and STO. And Kirkendall[16] and LeDoux[17] argued that ID tends to follow significant changes in the district population by as much as 6 to perhaps 10 or more years.[d] No research has been done, however, to directly investigate the total duration of either the episodes of instability or the (probably longer) periods of quiescence and policy stability.

A study by Mitchell and Thorsted[18] indicates that this lack of knowledge about the duration and/or spacing of episodic policy adjustments creates a significant problem for the interpretation of the lag-time data previously reported. The Mitchell-Thorsted analysis revealed that a district which has experienced an ID in one election is much more likely to have had an ID in the immediately previous election than is a district which has not. This finding confirms statistically what Iannaccone and Lutz discovered in Robertsdale: although an ID may reflect episodic political conflict, the episodes tend to involve an *extended* period covering more than one election in the life of a school district. This means that it is inappropriate to treat each ID as if it represented a separate episode of political upheaval. Defeats associated with continuing instability must be distinguishable from those representing the initial

---

[d]There are, no doubt, a host of unexplored variables which contribute to the speed with which dissatisfaction gets turned into policy changes. Some may operate in all districts, such as the length of board members' terms in office, the homogeneity of the community, and the normal length of superintendent contracts. Others will be situationally specific, such as the presence of effective political leaders or the saliency of the change issues, of the retirement of board members, or key staff in the district. As Garberina suggests, the response time of districts which are rising in socioeconomic status may differ significantly from that of those which are declining.

upsurge of dissatisfaction. The Iannaccone-Lutz model of school district politics is *testable* as a theory of democratic control only if the emergence of citizen dissatisfaction is clearly episodic—so that districts have identifiable periods of satisfaction with existing policy interrupted by limited periods of upheaval and change. If political conflict and upheaval leading to ID are distributed so that they are largely continuous in some districts and/or nearly nonexistent in others, it is impossible to test whether the upheaval or the stability is the result of changing citizen desires.[e]

The data presented in Eblen's[19] dissertation underscores this problem by showing how non-school-related sources of ID and uncertainty about the duration and spacing of change episodes can interact to complicate efforts to test the validity of the dissatisfaction theory of democratic control. As previously pointed out, Eblen could find no relationship between ID and STO in his data. However, the 37 districts in the sample did display a pattern of incumbent defeat which was significantly clustered by both time period and district type. His districts had significantly fewer (at the .01 level) incumbent defeats in the 1962-1967 period than in either of the 6-year periods before or after this time. His data also showed far fewer (significant at the .001 level) IDs in the 11 districts of his sample which were high in socioeconomic status (SES) and declining over the 1960-1970 period than in those which were lower in SES levels and were either stable or rising in status. Thus, if we had only Eblen's data to work from, we might easily conclude that ID arises from forces related to district SES characteristics, and perhaps some regional or national political mood, while being unable to relate ID to school policy change through STO. What is more likely, however, given the findings of the other studies, is that the Eblen data highlight the need for more sophisticated measurement and data analysis techniques—not a revised theory of democratic control. As will be discussed more fully in the fourth section, there is a substantial body of literature showing that districts with differing SES and political structure characteristics have a tendency to differ systematically in their levels of political conflict—including the likelihood that they will have different rates of ID. Furthermore, though these different patterns do not obviate dissatisfaction theory, they do call for increasingly sophisticated methods of study if this theory is to be thoroughly tested.

As Garberina[20] argues, school boards in districts with declining SES characteristics seem to respond more rapidly to dissatisfaction than those where SES levels are increasing. This makes it necessary to determine the direction as well as the magnitude of change in district SES in any effort to explain the relationship of board decisions to citizen interests.

---

[e]Of course, citizens in some districts may be continuously satisfied while others are virtually always dissatisfied. But if this is typically the case, then the loss of the essential *variability* in dissatisfaction makes statistical examination of its relation to governance impossible.

Variable Measurement Issues

No matter how sophisticated the theoretical foundations for a research effort become, research findings cannot be any more reliable than the indicators which are selected for measurement and the accuracy of the measurements taken on these indicators. In this section, four measurement issues related to the incumbent defeat-superintendent turnover strand of research are explored. The first two issues arise when an attempt is made to compare various research studies inspired by the work of Iannaccone and Lutz with research results found in other efforts to explain electoral conflict and policy change in school districts. These issues concern (1) measurement of electoral conflict within school districts and (2) measurement of socioeconomic status (SES) and political variables which influence or reflect the rate of dissatisfaction and conflict expressed in board elections. The third and fourth issues are more internal to research based on the dissatisfaction theory. The third issue concerns the possibility that dissatisfaction can be measured directly, rather than having to be inferred from changes in district population characteristics and behavior. The final measurement issue to be presented here addresses the problem of refining the measurement of incumbent defeat, the pivotal variable in this research strand.

Measuring Political Conflict

One frustrating problem encountered in trying to compare the findings generated by various research studies devoted to problems of electoral conflict in local school districts is that two quite different procedures for calculating an index of the amount of political conflict in a board election are present in the literature. One index was developed by David Minar[21] in his important studies of conflict in suburban school districts. Although Minar's conflict index has recently been criticized,[22] it has generally been utilized by researchers who hold competition. The Minar conflict index (MCI) is calculated by finding the percentage of the total vote cast in an election which goes to all the *losing* candidates. That is, the Minar conflict index is calculated from the following formula:

$$MCI = \left(\frac{\text{votes for losers}}{\text{total votes cast}} \right) \times 100$$

Researchers utilizing the dissatisfaction theory, however, generally have defined conflict—following Richard Kirkendall[23]—in terms of the divisions of votes between incumbent and nonincumbent candidates. Kirkendall himself had a rather complicated set of rules for determining the value of a conflict index. Thorsted,[24] however, modified Kirkendall's definition somewhat and then created a formula for calculating an index of conflict which can be easily derived and fruitfully compared with the Minar index. The Thorsted conflict index (TCI) measures the percentage of the total votes which are effectively cast *against* an incumbent school board by taking the ratio of the average number of votes received by each incumbent candidate to the average number of votes cast for each board seat being filled, and then subtracting this amount from 100 percent. That is, the formula for the Thorsted conflict index is

$$TCI = 100\% - 100 \times \left(\frac{\text{votes for all incumbents} \div \text{number of incumbents running}}{\text{total votes} \div \text{number of seats being filled}} \right)$$

Simple inspection of these two conflict index formulas will show why the Minar index tends to be preferred by competition theorists, while the Thorsted approach is preferred by dissatisfaction theory. First, note that as long as all incumbents run *and* they are all returned to office, the two indices have exactly the same value. This arises because the losing candidates are all nonincumbents in the Minar formula, while the variable term in the Thorsted index reduces to the percentage of votes cast for the (winning) incumbents. Of course, the percentage of vote for the losers is then just 100 percent minus the percentage for the winners.

In cases when all the incumbents run and all are defeated, the TCI will *always be larger* than the MCI. This occurs because the MCI treats votes for the (now losing) incumbents along with votes for other losers, while the TCI treats the votes for the winning nonincumbent candidates as part of the proportion of votes *not* cast for the incumbents and therefore indicative of dissatisfaction with incumbent school board.

The two indices differ, sometimes dramatically, whenever some but not all incumbents retire without seeking reelection and/or when some but not all are defeated. Under these circumstances the Thorsted index becomes larger than the Minar index if the winning incumbents get fewer votes than winning nonincumbents, and the Minar index is larger if winning incumbents lead the field.

From the perspective of dissatisfaction theory, the Thorsted index offers two distinct advantages. First, since the TCI separates the votes for incumbents from those for nonincumbents, it is more consistent in recording the level of opposition to the current school board which is being expressed in an election. Second, if the defeat of an incumbent is accepted as a solid indication that voters desire policy change in the district, then the TCI does a better job of consistently reflecting this desire. In the important cases, when all incumbents are being soundly defeated at the polls, the TCI continues to rise in value, while the MCI actually decreases in value as the defeat of the incumbents becomes more and more decisive.

Reanalysis of available data provides a ready test of the extent to which the Thorsted and the Minar indices adequately reflect the level of electoral dissent required to defeat incumbent school board members. In a sample of 198 elections in which incumbents sought reelection (drawn from the Thorsted and Kirkendall dissertations), a test was made of the reliability with which each conflict index was able to separate the elections involving incumbent defeat from those in which all incumbents seeking reelection won. Both indices successfully predicted the outcomes of 126 elections, while failing to predict 41 of the outcomes. The Thorsted index succeeded where the Minar index did not 29 times, while the MCI was superior only twice. This is significant well beyond the .001 level, indicating that the Thorsted index is not only theoretically superior as a measure of citizen dissatisfaction but also empirically superior as an index of actual electoral dissent.

The empirical superiority of the Thorsted index does not mean, however, that research findings utilizing the Minar index should be neglected entirely. Despite its weakness in reflecting conflict leading to ID, the Minar index does maintain a correlation of .70 ($p < .001$) with the Thorsted index, in comparing scores on these ID elections. Hence the findings by Minar and his followers which suggest that the level of electoral conflict in a school district is directly related to the socioeconomic and political variables (which do not change rapidly and which are probably not responsible for *changes* in citizen views on matters of school policy) must be taken seriously, if somewhat cautiously. This point will be discussed further in the fourth section when data analysis techniques which have the capacity to control for the effects of SES and political structure variables on the rate of ID and STO are discussed.

*Measuring Socioeconomic and Political Variables Related
to Dissatisfaction and Electoral Conflict*

As was pointed out in the second section, although dissatisfaction theory identifies citizen policy values or ideology as the ultimate cause of incumbent defeat and superintendent turnover in local school districts, no studies are yet available which have attempted to test statistical relationships between direct measures of dissatisfaction and ID or STO.[f] Instead, research following this theory has reasoned that changes in certain characteristics of the school district population could be taken as likely indicators that changes in the citizenry will be accompanied by changing views on policy. Thus, in mounting research efforts, dissatisfaction theorists have hypothesized that the following sequence of events occurs: (1) district population changes occur (perhaps through immigration, outmigration, annexation, or unification with other districts, or through

---

[f]Indirect suggesting that the superintendents' fate is closely tied to policy satisfaction is reasonably convincing. The works of Carlson and Reynolds, together with Walden's questions testing the policy basis for superintendent dismissal, seem quite solid in the absence of any contrary findings.

industrial or residential development in the district); (2) these changes in population are accompanied by changes in ideological commitments to schooling and school policy; (3) changed ideology leads to dissatisfaction with existing board and management policies; (4) because boards and superintendents are typically insensitive to these changed values, political action and conflict are required to secure policy changes; (5) the conflict leads to ID; (6) the ID leads to STO; and (7) the STO finally leads to significant changes in district policy and personnel.

There is a danger in this formulation, however, which must be carefully guarded against in the choice and measurement of indicators if results are to be trusted. Eblen has identified this danger quite clearly. Reviewing the work of Richard Kirkendall,[25] he claims that

Kirkendall's indicator was not a correct measure of Iannaccone and Lutz's concept. Kirkendall was only measuring the *amount* of conflict in the election prior to the one in which incumbent defeat occurred. But to properly test Iannaccone and Lutz, Kirkendall should have been measuring whether there were *changes* in the amount of conflict in the election prior to the incumbent defeat election. He thus did not have a correct measure of Iannaccone and Lutz's concept that there would be an increase in conflict levels prior to incumbent board member defeat.[26]

Although Eblen's effort to remedy this problem in Kirkendall's work, using the less reliable Minar conflict index as a measure of conflict, is also inappropriate as a test of the dissatisfaction model, his criticism is essentially correct. In fact, with regard to indicator measurement, this criticism brings the whole relationship between Iannaccone and Lutz's dissatisfaction theory and other models of school governance into proper perspective. Competition theorists, following Minar, have been intensely interested in the *amount* of political conflict generated by various school district processes and characteristics. The Iannaccone and Lutz line of research is (or at least ought to be) concerned with the *change* in electoral conflict which, along with other district indicators, reveals the connection between changes in the school district population's degree of satisfaction with school policy matters and the fate of the incumbent school board and superintendent.

The competition theorists have demonstrated convincingly that the general level of electoral competition is directly related to the general level of socioeconomic status within school districts which share the same political structure. Additionally, Zeigler and Jennings argue that the presence of such political reform structures, such as at-large or nonpartisan election procedures or holding school board elections separately from elections for other government officials, has an even more dramatic effect on the reduction of the general level of electoral conflict than does the socioeconomic level of the population.

There seems no immediate reason to doubt that both citizen dissatisfaction and socioeconomic and political structure variables affect the levels of electoral conflict and the probability of an ID within a school district. If, however, socioeconomic changes also indicate that ideological change is occurring among district voters, then careful measurements are needed in order to separate the direct effects of socioeconomic status changes on the level of conflict within a district from the indirect effects which these changes have on conflict through the emergence of dissatisfaction with existing policy. Once the background levels of political conflict and socioeconomic status variables are combined with adequate change measurements on these variables, it may turn out that democratic control (through the influence of dissatisfaction on incumbent board member defeat and superintendent turnover) may be even more powerful than has been thus far demonstrated. Or it may turn out that the process works better in districts with certain political or socioeconomic characteristics than in others. Effective tests of these possibilities remain to be undertaken.[g]

One reason why testing interaction between the *levels* of socioeconomic and political indicators and the *changes* in them is so difficult springs from the fact that school district boundaries do not generally conform either to those of other government units or to census tracts. The result of the uniqueness of school district boundaries is that gathering effective data on socioeconomic and political variables is tedious and expensive. A few researchers have followed Minar's lead in aggregating census data by school districts, but just as often the indicators of socioeconomic status have been drawn exclusively from the sorts of data typically kept by the school districts. This means that assessed valuation of district property has been the major socioeconomic variable, and it has been virtually impossible to get accurate data on such simple political variables as the rate of voter turnout for an election. Since the Iannaccone-Lutz model insists that it takes time for changed policy orientations to result in incumbent defeat and superintendent turnover, it is important that the data be longitudinal as well as comparative. This complicates still further the efforts to compare school district data with more traditional indicators of SES drawn from census data. While these problems are primarily practical rather than substantive, they have thus far prevented researchers from testing the dissatisfaction theory with the thoroughness which it deserves. They have made it virtually impossible to compare the effects of the non-school-related sources of electoral conflict, which have been of interest to competition theorists, with the dissatisfaction-based sources of political conflict, which are central to the Iannaccone-Lutz formulation of school governance theory. Furthermore, as can be seen from the material presented in chapter 2, the list of potentially important sociocultural variables is

---

[g]It is, of course, *possible* that the dependence of ID and STO on socioeconomic variables is not related to policy satisfaction at all. It may be that the changes which voters seek are related primarily to job opportunities or school construction or service contracts (after all, schooling is, often the largest industry within a district's boundaries); or the changes may be no more than a symbolic matter of new people wanting to put "one of their own" in a position of power.

far from complete. Researchers following this line of inquiry are in no danger of running out of work in the near future.

Direct Measurement of Ideological Orientation and
Citizen Dissatisfaction

Faced with these complex practical problems in data gathering, dissatisfaction theory research might profit from increased attention to the *direct* measurement of citizen dissatisfactions. ID-STO research hypothesizes that school political actions are informed by the value or ideological commitments of district residents and their leaders. From this hypothesis springs the corollary that the ID-STO process is carrying a mandate for change from the citizens into the school governance and management systems, a mandate which embodies the norms and values of the district residents. These hypotheses, however, have not been effectively studied because of an absence of suitable measurements for the school policy values embraced by citizens, board members, and/or school professionals. This has made it necessary to rely on the admittedly weak and possibly confounded indications of dissatisfaction and changed policy ideology found in demographic or electoral conflict changes in the district. A great leap forward in testing the Iannaccone-Lutz conceptualization of school governance could be made through the successful measurement of school policy commitments held by the citizens and their elected school boards and the resulting professional educator staff in the school districts.

A Q-sort instrument developed by Mitchell[27] has shown some promise as a measurement instrument for this purpose. In one study, this instrument was able to measure the school policy liberalism and conservatism of school board members and members of the community elites. More recently, Mitchell and Badarak[28] report that the instrument has successfully discriminated between former school board members who have suffered defeat and the successful insurgents who ousted them from the board. If adequate ideological measurements can be made, much of the uncertainty about whether changes in district political and socioeconomic characteristics are really indicative of changed orientations toward school-related policy matters can be removed. This is certainly an important direction for future research on the role of ID and STO in the process of school governance.

Measuring Incumbent Defeat

Although in their original statistical work on the relationship between ID and STO Walden[29] and Freeborn[30] were well aware that election outcomes were much more complex than a simple ID, no-defeat dichotomous variable indicates, not much has been done in later research to refine operational measurements of electoral instability since their initial work in this area. The original studies developed a 15-point scale of electoral instability which ranged from a score of 1 for elections in which all incumbents were reelected in an uncontested election to a score of 15 for a successful recall election in which two or more board members lost their seats. After developing this spectrum of possible levels of instability, however, Walden and Freeborn did not analyze any of its correlates. Instead they collapsed the scaled measurements on their 692 elections into a simple dichotomous defeat/no-defeat variable. A recent study by Mitchell and Thorsted,[31] however, provides some evidence that the Walden-Freeborn decision rules may not have been the best ones.[h]

By examining the number of candidates who ran for election in 312 elections held in 104 school districts, Mitchell and Thorsted were able to demonstrate that both dissatisfaction with the incumbent board—as reflected in incumbent defeats—*and* the opportunity for office presented by incumbent retirements tended to increase the number of nonincumbent candidates who run for office. Furthermore, when all incumbents retire simultaneously, the number of candidates tends to be as high as would be expected from both the dissatisfaction and the opportunity motives. Hence this study concluded that it is more appropriate to classify the simultaneous retirement of all incumbents as an unstable rather than a stable election. Of course, mistakes in classification will be made no matter which way the withdrawal of incumbents is treated. The Mitchell-Thorsted argument is simply that fewer mistakes result from considering these withdrawal situations as indicating "unstable" district politics and therefore likely to lead to superintendent turnover.[i]

Not only does it seem likely that some elections which do not involve the literal defeat of an incumbent are, nevertheless, best classified along with incumbent defeats as indicating voter dissatisfaction; there are also some elections in which the reverse is true. For example, of 20 incumbent defeat elections in 1973 found in Thorsted's data, 5 involved the defeat of board members who had been appointed since the last district election and were therefore standing for election for the first time. As the data presented in table 7-1 indicate, the amount of electoral conflict required to defeat these appointees is significantly lower than that required for defeating incumbents seeking reelection after having previously won their seat at the polls. In fact, the mean score for the Thorsted electoral conflict index for the five appointees did not differ significantly from the mean score for those elections which were contested without leading to an incumbent defeat.[j]

---

[h]Chapter 7 presents some work in which the voting result is treated as a continuous variable n rather than simply a matter of defeat or no defeat.

[i]In chapter 5 Burlingame also discuss this withdrawal phenomenon.

[j]In terms of the satisfaction theory of democracy, this finding simply suggests that board members may make mistakes in identifying satisfactory candidates, and when they do, the appointee has no better chance of winning than any candidate running for an open seat on the board.

Table 7-1
Comparison of Defeats for Appointees and Previously Elected Incumbents

	Defeated Previous Winners	Defeated Appointees
N	15	5
Thorsted Conflict Index Mean Score	52.60	39.40
(Standard Deviation)	(7.61)	(9.69)

t test for difference between mean scores: $t = 3.5$, $df = 18$ ($p < .005$).

Future work needs to be done on the possibility that a more refined operational definition of unstable "incumbent defeat" elections could be generated by using other variables in addition to the simple outcomes of the elections. In addition to determining whether an incumbent was appointed, how many nonincumbent challenges are seeking office, and whether multiple incumbents all withdraw without seeking reelection, the rate of voter turnout seems likely to reflect the level of dissatisfaction with the incumbent board (all other things being equal). If high voter turnout is associated with elections in which the incumbents are being rebuked by district voters, then this variable could be used for deciding which incumbent retirements are motivated by personal and which by political considerations. Also since the Minar strand of research finds that higher SES districts generally have lower levels of overall conflict, a high conflict index associated with incumbent withdrawal, or defeat of an appointed member seeking his/her first electoral victory, might be viewed as stronger evidence of a defeat for the incumbent board in the higher SES districts.

It is impossible to determine with any degree of certainty how much these refinements in the operational definition of a defeat for the incumbent board would affect previous research findings. One indication of the potential magnitude of the effects, however, can be seen by the fact that 25 percent of all the defeats in Thorsted's data for 1973 involved appointees and that there were nearly one-third as many complete withdrawals by incumbents as actual defeats in his entire sample. The combined impact of these refinements in the definition of incumbent defeat could alter significantly the picture of the relationship between ID, the SES and political characteristics of communities, and STO in school districts.

Data Analysis Issues

A review of local school district governance research methodology would not be complete without a careful look at the data analysis techniques used in various studies. Although much of the divergence in this research literature has arisen because researchers have had different theoretical interests or have utilized different measurement techniques, two problems arise related to difficulties encountered in the statistical analysis of data. First, in analyzing the relationship between school district socioeconomic and political variables and the occurrence of incumbent defeat, the major strands of research have tended to ignore the significance of one another's findings and have therefore tended to use statistically weak tools for hypothesis testing. Second, studies which have tried to examine the statistical relationship between ID and STO have had a tendency to use relatively weak tests which are statistically biased and which have resulted in an important oversight in the data interpretation.

Analyzing the Relationship between Governance Outcomes and Socioeconomic or Political Variables

In testing the relationships between governance outcomes and the socioeconomic or political characteristics of school districts, research based on the work of Minar (and testing some version of the competition theory of democratic control) has characteristically utilized correlational or multiple regression data analysis techniques. By contrast, except for Garberina,[32] those following Iannaccone and Lutz have utilized chi-square or multiple discriminant analysis. The difference between these two approaches is quite important in two respects.[33] First, they address different questions to the data; second, they differ in their ability to isolate and describe the effects of the various variables under investigation.

The use of multiple regression analysis by the competition theorists is very straightforward. They measure electoral outcomes, in terms of the electoral conflict present, by means of the Minar conflict index. This electoral conflict level is used as the *dependent* variable in the regression analysis, and an attempt is made to determine what socioeconomic and/or political variables are responsible for the level of conflict experienced. Multiple regression analysis is ideally suited for this task because it can very effectively determine which combination of independent variables best accounts for the variability in the electoral conflict scores. The problem with this approach, of course, is that it ignores the major hypothesis of the dissatisfaction theorists that the electoral conflict is itself only a mediating variable and that it is the actual defeat of incumbent board members and the ouster of the school superintendent which effectively control the process of school policy change.

Dissatisfaction theorists are interested in electoral conflict scores only to the extent that changes in electoral conflict are a part of the *pattern* of changes in school district citizen behavior which lead to ID and ultimately to significant policy shifts. Because the central interest is in incumbent defeat, which is a nominal variable with only the two categories of "defeat" and "no defeat" rather than an interval variable with an extended scale of possible scores, it was natural for Kirkendall,[34] in his original work, to think of multiple discriminant analysis as the appropriate statistical technique. The multiple discriminant approach, however, does not ask the most important question about the electoral outcome data. Especially in light of the competition theorists' finding that the rate of conflict—and probably also of incumbent defeat—depends upon certain SES and political characteristics in the school districts, the issue of interest is not merely whether the districts with and without incumbent defeats are significantly different.[35] The real question is whether the differences between ID and non-ID districts can be attributed to *particular* predictor variables which can be reasonably assumed to also reflect citizens' orientations toward existing school policy. Kirkendall and LeDoux[36] both recognized that this was the critical question, so they adopted the technique of repeatedly altering the set of predictor variables used in the discriminant analysis and then recalculating the discriminant function until a theoretically interesting and statistically manageable set of predictors remained which retained enough power to significantly separate the ID and the non-ID districts.

This discriminant analysis technique does not, however, assess whether each of the predictor variables remaining in any final discriminant function is significantly contributing to the ability of the function to reliably discriminate between the two groups of districts. Methodologically this is the great weakness of discriminant analysis—no standard statistical techniques have yet been developed which permit us to reliably determine which of a set of predictors are contributing significantly to the power of the function to discriminate among groups of school districts.[37] The best that is offered by statistical methodologists is the rule-of-thumb suggestion that the discriminant coefficient with the largest absolute magnitude—and any whose magnitude is as much as one-half the size of the largest coefficient—be used for interpreting the relative importance of various predictors. If this rule of thumb had been applied by Kirkendall, he would not have concluded that ID was dependent upon six, much less nine or more, variables, as he and those using his work as a foundation have been accustomed to doing. Only *two* coefficients in Kirkendall's final discriminant function would normally be utilized for interpreting the differences between his groups of districts. If discriminant analysis is to continue to be used for this research, the appropriate procedure is to continue to eliminate all variables until, in the final function, all of the coefficients are no smaller than one-half of the largest coefficient. Such a procedure is tedious, however, and does not tell us about the possible contributions of some variables whose impact may be highly *significant* in accounting for the occurrence of ID, but whose impact on the total rate of ID is not very large.

Garberina's research (summarized in chapter 6) has left the less adequate discriminant analysis approach and turned to a multiple regression technique for data analysis. With this approach he is able to identify the variables which make the strongest contribution to the occurrence of ID within school districts. This is an important step forward. Garberina, however, still focuses his attention on making global distinctions between the different types of districts in his sample, rather than on isolating the variables which make significant contributions to the occurrence of incumbent defeats and determining whether those statistically significant variables are more compatible with competition or dissatisfaction theories of democratic control.

In the future an effort needs to be made to identify those SES and political variables which are responsible for the *base levels* of conflict and defeat and to separate these from variables which reflect *changes* in district populations and their orientations toward school policy. The first group of variables, then, needs to be used as covariates so as to statistically control the effects of base-level characteristics; then the second set of variables can be used to test the ability of dissatisfaction theory to explain the role of incumbent defeat in school governance. This calls for the use of multiple analysis of covariance, or at least stepwise regression with the base-level variables entered first into the equation so that an explanation of changes in the rate of ID arises from analysis of the residuals after the effects of base-rate variables have been removed.[38]

The Relationship between ID and STO

Certainly the central finding for all the episodic dissatisfaction research studies has been that superintendent turnover is directly dependent upon the occurrence of incumbent board member defeat in a local school district. It is only appropriate, therefore, to conclude this exploration of methodological and measurement issues with a brief review of the data analysis techniques used to test this relationship.

As was pointed out in the second section of this chapter, available research findings on the relationship between ID and STO are not consistent. Walden[39] and Freeborn[40] claimed a general dependence of STO on ID, but they used a complicated and unorthodox chi-square procedure for testing this relationship. Moen[41] only claims a connection between *involuntary* turnover and the defeat of school board members. When his data on all turnovers are collected, his method of chi-square analysis does not support the conclusion that IDs affect the general rate of superintendent departure from school districts. Eblen,[42] using longitudinal data but applying the same type of chi-square test used in the Moen study, concludes that there is no evidence to support a conclusion that STO rates are affected by IDs.[k]

Careful review of the data analysis techniques used in these three studies

---

[k]Across the entire set of 317 districts in three states examined by Walden and Freeborn, Moen, and Eblen, there was an average of 38.22 superintendent turnovers per year, or approximately one every 9 years in the typical district. Of this number there wre only 19.55 *involuntary* turnovers per year, or only about one every 17 years represents vigorous democratic control for the schools.

show that their divergent findings are more likely to be the result of weak data analysis procedures than differences in the data itself. The problem, quite simply, is this: the chi-square contingency analysis used in each of these three studies to test whether STO follows within 3 (or 4) years of an ID election violates the conditions required for the appropriate application of chi-square analysis in two basic ways (see Lewis and Burke for the classic discussion of chi square).[43] First, chi-square contingency tests require that all observations being entered into the contingency table be drawn *independently*. That is, each observation must be made in such a way that it does not depend upon any other observation. This is not the case in either the Walden-Freeborn or the Eblen data. These two studies utilized the election histories of the districts in their samples over a period of several years. Since ID in one election increases the likelihood that there will be IDs in other elections in the same district, these repeated observations in the same districts violate the requirement of independent observations.

The second condition which must be met in order for a chi-square test to be valid is that all events which are being observed must have a chance of occurring in the data gathered which is equal to their proportional frequency in the total population. Since, however, it is hypothesized in the ID-STO research that a turnover may follow an ID by a period of *any length* up to 3 or 4 years, this condition is violated in all three studies reported. The Moen study violates this condition by observing only one election, and thus not observing elections which might easily have been responsible for many of the turnovers which he observed to occur as much as 3 years later. The longitudinal data in the Walden-Freeborn and Eblen data sets violate the same condition, though somewhat less severely, because they cannot record all the elections prior to each observed STO *and* also the turnovers in all the 3- or 4-year periods following each election. Only under the extremely unlikely situation where no STO occurs in the first 4 years and no ID occurs in the last 4 years of an observation period would the type of longitudinal data used in these studies *not* violate the second condition as well as the first.

The solution to this data analysis dilemma is actually quite simple, and it yields a fascinating new insight into the relationship between ID and STO. By using a three-way analysis of variance design, the interdependence and unequal probability of the observations can be controlled, and an unbiased test of the probability that STO is affected by ID can be made. A reanalysis of the Walden-Freeborn data will serve to illustrate the application of this analysis-of-variance procedure. The procedure is as follows. First, create a $117 \times 8 \times 2$, three-way analysis-of-variance data table with each row containing the observations from one of the 117 districts in the Walden-Freeborn data, each column containing observations of whether or not superintendent turnover occurs in each of the 8 years following an election (fewer years of observation are, of course, made on the later elections), and the two blocks containing, respectively, observations following ID elections and those following non-ID elections within the districts. Second, into each of the cells of this data table enter a score for each of the years, following each of the elections, in each of the districts. If the election involved ID, make the entries in the first block of the design; if it involved no ID, make the entries in the second block. Enter a score of 0.0 in each year when no STO occurred and a score of 1.0 in each year when STO did occur.[1] Finally, perform an analysis of variance on the completed data set. Table 7-2 presents the findings from the reanalysis of the Walden-Freeborn data using this procedure.

As this table reveals, there is a significant main effect from both districts and types of election outcomes. The significant main effect for the districts confirms the impropriety of the chi-square contingency analysis for this problem since it demonstrates that there is a significant tendency for STOs to be clustered in some and not other districts; hence repeated observations in each district are correlated, violating one of the chi-square test assumptions.[m] The significant main effect for election outcomes reconfirms, nevertheless, the validity of the earlier finding that more STOs occur in the years following ID elections than in the years after non-ID elections. The analysis-of-variance

Table 7-2
Three-way Analysis of Variance on the Rate of Superintendent Turnover Found by Walden and Freeborn[a]

Source	Sums of Squares	df	Mean Square	F	p
Districts	41.0565	116	.3539	3.00*	< .001
Election Outcome	1.6997	1	1.6997	14.42*	< .001
Years	.3180	7	.0454	.385	n.s.
Districts × Outcome	.5461	116	.0047	.040	n.s.
Districts × Years	39.8088	812	.0490	.416	n.s.
Outcome × Years	1.0246	7	.1464	1.242	n.s.
Districts × Outcome × Years	55.0403	812	.0678	.575	n.s.
Within Cells	306.1167	2597	.1179		
Total	445.6107	4468			

[a]Factors are districts, years following elections, and type of election outcome (ID or non-ID); dependent variable is superintendent turnover (scored 1.0 or 0.0).

[1]Although STO is a nominal variable, it has only two levels ("turnover" and "no turnover"). Therefore it can be treated by the same statistical procedures as are appropriate to internal-level variables with no loss in the reliability of the findings.

[m]As noted earlier, the IDs are also clustered in certain districts. While it might seem reasonable to *assume* that the clustering of IDs and STOs is the result of dissatisfaction, it is just this assumption which we are attempting to test; it is therefore necessary to find a statistical method which controls for possible correlation among observations—one which does not require that we assume what we are trying to test.

procedure allows us to go further, however, and to examine how long after an ID occurs the STO is likely to follow. While the chi-square contingency test forced Walden and Freeborn (and their successors) to guess at the length of time required for the ID to eventuate in the change of superintendents, the analysis-of-variance approach outlined here provides a year-by-year estimate of the rate of STO following each election type. Figure 7-1 presents a graph of the rate of STO over the first 8 years following both ID and non-ID elections observed by Walden and Freeborn. As the graph clearly demonstrates, there are *two* separate peaks in the rate of STO following ID. The first peak comes in the second year, and another slightly smaller peak occurs in the fifth year following the ID. Planned-contrast analysis-of-variance tests confirm statistically what the graph depicts: only in the second and fifth year following each type of election outcome is the rate of STO significantly higher for elections resulting in ID. We can confidently conclude from this analysis that either a superintendent tends to fall victim to the press for a change by a successful insurgent board member during the second year of that new board member's tenure or the superintendent is relatively safe until the insurgent is reelected for a second term (note that these data were taken from California school districts where board members serve 4-year terms, with elections held every 2 years for approximately one-half of the board seats).[n] Apparently the legitimacy of some victorious insurgent board members is successfully questioned by the "old guard" board members and the superintendent they have appointed. Under these circumstances, the

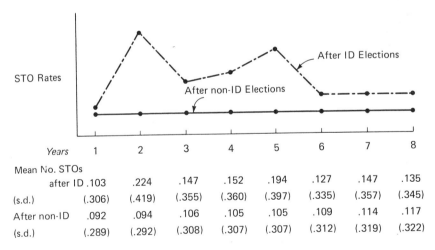

Years	1	2	3	4	5	6	7	8
Mean No. STOs after ID	.103	.224	.147	.152	.194	.127	.147	.135
(s.d.)	(.306)	(.419)	(.355)	(.360)	(.397)	(.335)	(.357)	(.345)
After non-ID	.092	.094	.106	.105	.105	.109	.114	.117
(s.d.)	(.289)	(.292)	(.308)	(.307)	(.307)	(.312)	(.319)	(.322)

Figure 7-1. Superintendent Turnover Rates Following ID and Non-ID Elections

[n]Note that the fifth-year peak could not result from *additional* IDs at the end of the insurgent's first term, for these IDs would be followed by STO in their *first* year—and the first year rate of STO is not significantly above the rate for elections not involving IDs.

reelection of the insurgent apparently removes all doubt of his or her legitimate representation of a desire for change, and he or she is able to send the superintendent on his/her way.

Summary

The analysis of issues arising from (1) the theoretical bases of governance research, (2) problems in variable measurement, and (3) difficulties in data analysis presented above not only points to new directions for research in this area but also tends to suggest that the Iannaccone-Lutz model is even stronger than present research would indicate. This analysis continues to affirm that democratic control of local school district policy formation operates through the influence of citizen dissatisfaction on electoral outcomes and superintendent careers.

Notes

1. Laurence Iannaccone and Frank W. Lutz, *Politics, Power and Policy: The Governing of Local School Districts* (Columbus, Ohio: Charles E. Merrill, 1970).

2. Harmon L. Zeigler, Kent M. Jennings with Wayne G. Peak, *Governing American Schools: Political Interactions in Local School Districts* (North Scituate, Mass.: Duxbury Press, 1974).

3. Iannaccone and Lutz, *Politics, Power and Policy.*

4. Frederick M. Wirt (ed.), *The Polity of the School* (Lexington, Mass.: D.C. Heath Co., 1975).

5. David W. Minar, "Educational Decision Making in Suburban Communities," Cooperative Research Project No. 2440 (Evanston, Ill.: Northwestern University, 1966).

   David W. Minar, "The Community Basis of Conflict in School System Politics," *American Sociological Review*, vol. 31, no. 6 (December 1966), pp. 822-34.

   David W. Minar, "Community Politics and School Boards," *American School Board Journal*, vol. 154, no. 3 (March 1967), pp. 33-38.

6. Zeigler and Jennings, *Governing American Schools.*

7. Iannaccone and Lutz, *Politics, Power and Policy.*

8. Richard D. Carlson, *Executive Succession and Organizational Change* (Chicago: Midwest Administrative Center, University of Chicago, 1962).

   Richard D. Carlson, *Adoption of Educational Innovations* (Eugene, Ore.: Center for Advanced Study of Educational Administration, 1965).

   Richard D. Carlson, *School Superintendents: Careers and Performance* (Columbus, Ohio: Charles E. Merrill, 1968).

9. J.A. Reynolds, "Innovation Related to Administrative Tenure, Succession and Orientation: A Study of the Adoption of New Practices by School Systems," Ed.D. dissertation, St. Louis: Washington University, 1965.

10. Iannaccone and Lutz, *Politics, Power and Policy.*

11. John C. Walden, "School Board Changes and Involuntary Superintendent Turnovers," Ph.D. dissertation, Claremont Graduate School, 1966.

12. Robert M. Freeborn, "School Board Change and the Succession Pattern of Superintendents," Ph.D. dissertation, Claremont Graduate School, 1966.

13. Walden, "School Board Changes."

14. Allen W. Moen, "Superintendent Turnover as Predicted by School Board Incumbent Defeat in Pennsylvania's Partisan Elections," Ph.D. dissertation, Pennsylvania State University, 1971.

15. David R. Eblen, "School District Conflict and Superintendent Turnover in Transitional Suburban Communities," Ph.D. dissertation, University of Chicago, 1975.

16. Richard S. Kirkendall, "Discriminating Social, Economic, and Political Characteristics of Changing Versus Stable Policy-Making Systems in School Districts," Ph.D. dissertation, Claremont Graduate School, 1966.

17. Eugene P. LeDoux, "Outmigration: Its Relation to Social, Political and Economic Conditions and the Governing of Local School Districts in New Mexico," Ph.D. dissertation, University of New Mexico, Albuquerque, 1971.

18. Douglas E. Mitchell and Richard R. Thorsted, "Incumbent School Board Member Defeat Reconsidered: New Evidence for Its Political Meaning," *Educational Administration Quarterly* (Fall 1976) (in press).

19. Eblen, "School District Conflict."

20. William L. Garberina, Sr., "Public Demand, School Board Response and Incumbent Defeat: An Examination of the Governance of Local School Districts in Massachusetts," unpublished Ph.D. dissertation, Pennsylvania State University, 1975.

21. Minar, "Educational Decision Making"; "The Community Basis of Conflict."

22. Christine H. Rossell, "School Desegregation and Electoral Conflict," in Frederick M. Wirt (ed.), *The Polity of the School* (Lexington, Mass.: D.C. Heath Co., 1975).

23. Kirkendall, "Discriminating Social, Economic and Political Characteristics."

24. Richard R. Thorsted, "Predicting School Board Member Defeat: Demographic and Political Variables that Influence Board Elections," Ph.D. dissertation, University of California, Riverside, 1974.

25. Kirkendall, "Discriminating Social, Economic and Political Characteristics."

26. Eblen, "School District Conflict," p. 69.

27. Douglas E. Mitchell, "Ideological Structure and School Policy-Making," Ph.D. dissertation, Claremont Graduate School, 1972.

28. Douglas E. Mitchell and Gary W. Badarak, "Political Ideology and School Board Politics" (forthcoming).

29. Walden, "School Board Changes."

30. Freeborn, "School Board Change."

31. Mitchell and Thorsted, "Incumbent School Board Member Defeat Reconsidered."

32. Garberina, "Public Demand, School Board Response and Incumbent Defeat."

33. Norman H. Nie, Hadlai C. Hull, Jean G. Jenkins, Karin Steinbrenner, and Dale H. Bent, *Statistical Package for the Social Sciences*, 2d ed. (New York: McGraw-Hill Book Co., 1975).

Richard J. Harris, *A Primer of Multivariate Statistics* (New York: Academic Press, Inc., 1975).

Hubert M. Blalock, Jr., *Causal Inferences in Nonexperimental Research* (New York: W.W. Norton & Co., 1972) (Originally published in 1961).

34. Kirkendall, "Discriminating Social, Economic and Political Characteristics."

35. Ibid.

36. LeDoux, "Outmigration."

37. Maurice M. Tatsuoka, *Discriminant Analysis: The Study of Group Differences* (Champaign, Ill.: Institute for Personality and Ability Testing, 1970).

38. Chester W. Harris (ed.), *Problems in Measuring Change* (Madison, Wis.: University of Wisconsin Press, 1962).

39. Walden, "School Board Changes."

40. Freeborn, "School Board Change."

41. Moen, "Superintendent Turnover."

42. Eblen, "School District Conflict."

43. Don Lewis and C.J. Burke, "The Use and Misuse of the Chi-Square Test," *Psychological Bulletin*, vol. 46, no. 6 (November 1949), pp. 433-89.

References

William L. Boyd, "Community Status, Citizen Participation in Suburban School Politics," Ph.D. dissertation, University of Chicago, 1973.

William L. Boyd, "Community Status and Conflict in Suburban School Politics," Sage Professional Paper, American Politics Series, Series no. 04-025, vol. 3 (Beverly Hills, California: Sage Publications, 1976).

Peter J. Cistone (ed.), *Understanding School Boards: Problems and Prospects* (Lexington, Mass.: D.C. Heath Co., 1975).

Robert L. Crain, *The Politics of School Desegregation* (Chicago: Aldine Publishing Co., 1968).

Thomas E. Eliot, "Toward an Understanding of Public School Politics," *American Political Science Review*, vol. 53, no. 4 (December 1959), pp. 1032-51.

David J. Kirby, Robert T. Harris, Robert L. Crain, and Christine H. Rossell, *Political Strategies in Northern School Desegregation* (Lexington, Mass.: Lexington Books, D.C. Heath Co., 1973).

Eugene P. LeDoux and Martin Burlingame, "The Iannaccone-Lutz Model of School Board Change: A Replication in New Mexico," *Educational Administration Quarterly*, vol. 9 (Autumn 1973), pp. 48-65.

Frank W. Lutz, "The Role of Explanatory Models in Theory Building: In Response to LeDoux-Burlingame," *Educational Administration Quarterly*, vol. 11 (Winter 1965), pp. 72-78.

Douglas E. Mitchell, "Ideology and Public School Policy-Making," *Urban Education* vol. 9 (April 1974), pp. 35-59.

Allen W. Moen, "The Effect of Partisan Elections on the Incumbent Defeat-Superintendent Turnover Relationship," Paper presented at the AERA annual meeting (San Francisco, California, April 1976).

David O'Shea, "School Board-Community Relations and Local Resource Utilization," unpublished doctoral dissertation, University of Chicago, 1971.

Frederick M. Wirt and Michael W. Kirst, *Political and Social Foundations of Education* Berkeley, Calif.: McCutchan, 1972).

8 Beyond Operational Indicators—Toward Explanatory Relationships

Introduction

The entire thrust of the research and theory presented in this book is based on the premise and observation that during identifiable periods of time and under certain circumstances a local school board behaves in a particular fashion. As boards develop public policy in education, there results considerable citizen dissatisfaction, community-board conflict, incumbent school board member defeat, and superintendent turnover. Additionally, as this series of events is played out in the politics of education, the succession of the new superintendent provides an opportunity and mandate for policy changes, which brings about a policy output more in line with community aspirations and desires, resulting in a new period of equilibrium. Thus, the series of events describe a theory of democratic political process that can and in fact does require responsiveness within public education.

The specific indicators (social, economic, political indicators of community change and response indicators of the local board) are symptomatic of the condition and not likely causative. To put it another way, these indicators can be shown to be related to incumbent defeat and superintendent turnover, but no one really expects that those variables are the ones that affect or cause the conflict and political changes.

Explanatory Relationships

Theoretically, the process operates in approximately the following fashion. For a period of time a school board and its chief administrator operate in their policy output and implementation in a fashion that is satisfactory or at least reasonably noncontroversial for the majority of the citizens of the district. Then for some reason the public begins to ask for and finally demand certain policy changes. Operating in typical fashion, the board and the administration reject these attempts to influence and bring about change. As these attempts are unsuccessful the public becomes increasingly frustrated and discontented. Finding no way to influence the incumbent school board, the public moves in increasing numbers to the voting booth in an effort to elect board members who will represent the public's point of view in public policy decisions. The question remains, however, as to why school boards appear to be so impervious to public desires and attempts to influence their decisions, short of incumbent defeat.

101

Blanchard[1] has pointed out that the vast majority of school board members believe that they are under no obligation to behave as school board members, based on the wishes of the public. He found that 87 percent of the school board members he surveyed in Kentucky said they voted as they felt best even if that was opposed to what the public wished. This finding was substantiated in Pennsylvania by the work of Edgren.[2] On the surface such behavior is difficult to account for, coming from public officials who depend on the ballot box for their office. Given this condition, it is easier to explain the incumbent defeat phenomena than it is to explain why it takes so long to occur.

The Culture of School Boards

Lutz[3] attempted to explain the conditions that lead to and support this nonresponsiveness of school boards by positing a culture of school boards. He suggested that, over the last century, a set of norms, values, beliefs, and expectations has developed about school boards and their members. These are widely shared, supported by the literature in school administration and school boards and the precepts of reform government in education. Thus, the culture of school boards holds that education is too important to become a political affair and that school board members are trustees for the public, not representatives of the public. New school board members are acculturated, upon their election, through a planned process that inducts them into the culture of school boards and transforms them into "true believers." The norms of the culture instruct the board member to avoid representing any group within the school district and to do what is good for every pupil in spite of the wide differences in needs, aspirations, culture, ability, and desires within the population. Since most school board members are drawn from the middle and upper classes of the society, school board policy, operating in such a fashion and based on what the board thinks best, is likely to enhance middle- and upper-class "mainstream America" and disadvantage others.

Additionally, seeking to operate in trusteeship for a public it assumes to be monolithic, the board is admonished by its cultural norms to seek consensus in private and to avoid public conflict and the public debate of controversial issues. Thus, those who attempt to influence school boards in directions other than those school boards are predisposed to take, find their efforts thwarted. Most often such persons and groups are labeled as malcontents and not representative of the generalized public. If the change-oriented public finds an occasional friend on the board, that member can be expected to represent the public's view in private session, but retire in favor of the majority board opinion, and in order to preserve consensus (which the culture demands) vote against the public's wishes in public sessions. Is it any surprise that the public feels unrepresented?

As community pressure builds, some board members begin to lose confidence in the administration, which is almost their sole source of information and alternatives, but they remain "true believers" in the norms of the culture. This condition generates conflict within the board as well as between the board and the community. But no alternatives exist within the culture of school boards. The board is still compelled to reach consensus, act only on administratively proposed recommendations, and behave as trustees rather than representatives. Research based on a model provided by F.G. Bailey[4] has provided some tentative answers to the process of dissatisfaction and political action described above.

Elite and Arena Councils

Bailey and several of his colleagues in political anthropology have studied governing councils (other than school boards), using a model of council behavior that is described on a continuum from elite to arena council behavior.[5] The two councils were distinguished as follows:

Elite Councils:

1. Reach decisions in private, the minority acceding to the majority to preserve consensus, and enact the decision in public by unanimous vote
2. Think of themselves as trustees, apart from and separate from the public for whom they are the guardians of the trusteeship
3. Operate with the executive-administrative function being an integrated part of the council so that consensus is required if anything is to get done

Arena Councils:

1. Debate issues publicly and decide publicly by majority vote
2. Think of themselves as representatives of the public and act as "community in council"
3. Constitute the executive function apart from the council, holding administration responsible for effecting the majority decision

Any council, including school boards, can be placed on a continuum ranging from more elite to more arena. It seems clear that elite council behavior is dictated by the culture of school boards and that the great majority of school boards function as elite councils.

Anomic School Boards

During a 6-month study of two school boards, using participant/observer methods, Gresson[6] observed an elite and an arena school board. He discovered that things went smoothly in the elite board. There was little community conflict and no conflict within the board. When community pressure was brought to bear on the board or the superintendent, there was complete solidarity and protection of each individual and the decision-making body, including the superintendent. Additionally, the superintendent often acted for the board, thus "saving" the board the problem of making the decision.

In the arena board there was considerable intraboard conflict. Issues were debated publicly. Decisions were made by nonunanimous votes. There was constant conflict between the board and the superintendent. Community-board conflict was high; in fact, the community conflict was the major factor in producing the arena-type behavior. Because of the wide disagreements among segments of the public, certain board members no longer felt they could defend consensus on the board nor engage in blind support of the superintendent. Still locked in the culture of school boards, however, this arena board felt very uneasy about their inability to reach consensus and their lack of complete trust of the superintendent. They often expressed their unhappiness with this condition. They said they really did not think of themselves as representatives of the public and often were unsure of how to behave in board meetings. This condition was identified as anomic behavior, lacking in norms that sanctioned, supported, or guided their behavior.

Some descriptive material selected for the ethnography of the two districts may prove instructive to the understanding of the dissatisfaction process. Both school districts were essentially rural and encompassed large geographic areas. The socioeconomic status of the districts was similar, with the composition of the school boards being above in SES that of the generalized communities. The SES composition of the arena board, exhibiting the greatest conflict, was somewhat higher than that of the elite board.

The following quotes are typical of the behaviors and values expressed within the elite school board.

Given a particular request that a somewhat dissatisfied group in the community had made of the board, the superintendent in the elite board made an "administrative" decision and communicated that he "knew what the board wanted," and if it came to a board vote, the public would "get it out in the open and argue about it and maybe get their [the public group] way."

Such action was supported by the elite board who accepted the superintendent as a quasi-member of the board. One board member indicated, "That's one thing. We rely on Dr. John [the superintendent] and his staff. . . . It's [making policy decisions] a bigger job than most of us have time to give it."

Regarding consensus and unanimity of votes, one elite board member reported, "We never try to reach consensus . . . , But when you get nine people around the table discussing an issue, it doesn't take long to recognize how everyone feels about a thing. . . . If we see a thing is going to be problematic, we just don't bring it up in a [public] meeting. We just leave it. When we bring it up [in a public meeting], we know it is going to pass." Another member said, "Sometimes a guy will vote that way [against a majority decision] if one of his constituents is present. But he will only do that if he knows the motion is going to pass. You'll never see a fight or conflict. We always vote together. We meet in executive session."

Such norms, values, and behavior are descriptive of the elite-sacred-reform structure that prevails in most school districts. The strange thing is that these values were not related to the SES of the district nor the board members in the study. Over time such behavior may become less satisfying in lower-class communities (because the values of the board are often related to their relatively higher SES reference groups). These values and behaviors almost never appear to be in conflict with the school board itself, as demonstrated by the following data from the arena board.

Although neither the arena board nor its community differed significantly in SES composition from the elite board, its behavior was certainly different. Forced by community conflict to arena behavior, one arena board member reported, "I refuse to discuss anything in private. . . . I don't think that's fair to the public. . . . [It] wouldn't bother me in the least if every decision was a 5-4 vote . . . but I feel that most members would prefer a 9-0 decision." But even this member did not think of himself as a representative of the people. He said, "I don't vote in a certain way [as a representative of a public]. I explain to them why I don't feel this is a problem. I am a board member for the [entire] district."

Other board members felt very uneasy about this nonconsensus, nonunanimous voting behavior. Many reported an uneasiness and frustration about the situation. One said, "Just when you think you can rely on a board member, they go right in there and vote differently than you had agreed."

While none of the arena board supported a norm of public representation and few supported the notion of public debate or nonunanimous voting, almost all had grown to distrust the superintendent and no longer thought of him as a quasi-member of the board. They were not happy about this situation, however. A member of the press who had covered school board meetings for years commented, "The board would like to trust the superintendent, but he lies." An influential member of the teaching staff perhaps summed up the situation in the arena district by saying, "The board has a past orientation, some present, and very little future. They don't like to fight, but lately there has been a lot of 5-4 decisions. . . . It's revolving around the superintendent whom they want to get rid of." Such a lack of future orientation is symptomatic of an anomic society. Following the theory of such societies, it was suggested that this board was organizationally suicidal and that incumbents would soon be replaced and the superintendent would soon lose his job. Both predictions were borne out within the year.

Studying 30 selected school boards in Pennsylvania, Witmer[7] statistically identified five anomic school boards. These boards were all at least 1.5 standard deviations above the mean of the 30 boards in the number of decisions made by nonunanimous votes. They tended to be arena boards as they did not decide by consensus. However, they continued to express the elite norms of being trustees rather than representatives of the public, believing that they *should* obtain consensus (although they tended not to) and being uneasy about their lack of complete confidence in and support of their superintendent. Their scores on the elite-arena value scale were 1.5 standard deviations from the mean of the 30 boards and toward the elite value end of the scale. Apparently these boards, although arena boards, still believed in the norms, values, and customs dictated by the culture of school boards but found themselves unable to live according to these norms. They can be termed as *anomic*, and one can predict incumbent defeat and superintendent turnover in these districts.

An Explanatory Model of Conflict and Political Defeat

Perhaps the above descriptions are instructive in making clinical guesses about possible explanatory relationships within the dissatisfaction theory of local governance. The following statements seem descriptive of this process:

1. There is a culture of school boards that dictates that school boards operate in elite fashion.

This culture has developed in response to the drive for reform government in education. That movement has tended to remove public policy in education from the general politics of American democracy. It has established an elite system of decision making seated within a system of select trustees and professionals, deliberately removed from the direct influence of the people. It has cultivated a set of deeply held beliefs, norms, values, and behaviors, making school board members trustees and guardians for the people who believe they know better than the people and know what is best for the people about matters in public education. The culture denigrates any board member who attempts to represent a group of citizens, labeling such board members as low-level politicians uninterested in "good" education. Within this culture school boards have little choice but to function as elite boards. When forced to arena behavior, they become normless and anomic.

2. Given the diversity of the public which many school boards serve or the likelihood that the public changes over a period of time, it is unlikely that any single decision will be satisfactory to everyone or that a single point of view about public education will be satisfying over long periods.

The American society is multicultural, holding different values, abilities, backgrounds, and aspirations and often having widely different needs. Even the most homogeneous community occasionally changes because of in-migration or out-migration, changing property values, and economic shifts, to mention but a few indices. The consensual decision made by the best-intentioned school board is hardly likely, under these circumstances, to satisfy all persons or groups in most communities, particularly diverse cosmopolitan, urban communities. Yet those who feel disadvantaged by the consensual decision see no one who can or wants to support their position or meet their needs; and they have little hope of influencing the present school board.

3. Included in the culture of school boards is the superintendent. Neither the board nor the superintendent see themselves, nor are they viewed by the public, as independent in the process of the policy-making implementation.

The public views policy decisions as the combined operational output of the board and the superintendent. If the decisions are good, if they are satisfied, the board and the superintendent are good. The antithesis is also true. When the output is bad, both the board and the superintendent are bad.

4. Having little or no influence on the present school board and seeing no apparent opportunity to change that situation, the public will turn to the ballot box in an effort to unseat an incumbent and elect a board member who represents the public's position.

This represents the focal point of the dissatisfaction theory of democratic participation in school governance. Regardless of the sacred and protective nature of local school governance, most school boards are elected. When dissatisfaction and influence cannot be made operational through other means, the ballot box remains. Given the culture of school boards and the elite council behavior it dictates, incumbent defeat is often the only effective means of influence, in fact the means of last resort. Frustrated with their failure to influence the present board, groups seek and elect individuals to the board who, they think, will better represent their point of view when enacting public policy in education. Given that these new members will soon be acculturated, believing in the values of the culture of the school board, the public will, after time, again be faced with the same problem.

5. Since the public, the board, and the superintendent view the board and the superintendent as one impregnable decision-making system, a new school board member elected because of this dissatisfaction process will normally carry a mandate to "get rid" of the present superintendent.

This postulate requires little explanation. Since school board policy making tends to be an elite process, requiring the confidence and consent of all the school board *and* the superintendent, nothing is likely to change until a new superintendent is on the scene. The arrival of a new superintendent provides the opportunity for a policy shift toward the norms, values, and aspirations of the insurgent group who thought themselves disadvantaged by the old system and were successful in ousting an incumbent or several incumbents on the old board.

These five postulates describe the explanatory interrelationships underlying the dissatisfaction theory of democratic participation in local school governance. They rest within a theory of culture, culture conflict, and culture change. The critical factor is a culture of the school board which does not permit school board members to even think of themselves as representatives of the pluralistic public, much less act as their representatives. As long as the culture of school boards continues to exist unamended, an effective process of participation will continue through public dissatisfaction and frustration with attempts to influence political action at the polls, resulting in incumbent defeat and superintendent turnover. If and when the culture of school boards is amended to permit arena behavior, without creating an anomic condition on the school board, this dissatisfaction theory will have to be amended also. Until then it appears to account for conflict in, and be the most effective means of, public participation in local school policy making.

Other Explanations

Certain other theories of politics in local schools have attempted to account for democratic participation and conflict in educational politics. Dale Mann[8] has suggested a process of public participation and administrative representation in the formulation of local educational policy. This administrative representation theory views the school administration, particularly the principal, as someone who may represent the public served by the local school. While accounting for many interesting variables in the schooling process, the theory has failed, in our view, to recognize one important fact. School principals are *not* elected officials. They might better be viewed as the appointed ward and precinct delegates of the power wielders of the sacred political machine governing the local schools. In this sense we *do not* use the term *machine* to refer to an immoral, self-seeking, boss-dominated and politically corrupt, party-oriented government. Rather it refers to a system that produces policy decisions and programs in a bureaucratic and machinelike fashion.

If principals are the appointed officers of the machine, the extent to which they can represent the public, in opposition to the policies of the machine, good or bad, is problematic. The power group, the machine—the school board and superintendent in this case—can and often does replace the principal (the precinct leader) who insists on representing a group of people in opposition to the policies of the school board. Where does this leave the public and the principal? The principal looks for a new job, and the public is again forced to express their dissatisfaction at the ballot box.

David Minar[9] has shown that conflict in local school politics is related to the socioeconomic status of the school district. Specifically, Minar's work demonstrates that local school districts comprised of individuals of lower socioeconomic status experience more conflict than those districts comprised of individuals of higher SES. Minar also showed that such conflict increased over time and often led, eventually, to incumbent board member defeat and superintendent turnover. Thus, Minar's research parallels and supports, in some aspects, the dissatisfaction theory of local school politics. It does not account, however, for such a procedure in relatively higher SES districts except that, as Minar points out, higher SES communities have other mechanisms for handling conflict, participating in policy making, and formulating policy changes.

In addition to this explanation, as pointed out by Banfield and Wilson,[10] middle- and upper-class values are more oriented to the reform government process described earlier in local school districts, while lower-class persons have never found reform government to be very responsive to their needs. Perhaps this is but another way of saying the same thing.

Boyd[11] has noted such differences in the political culture of higher and lower SES districts and demonstrated that both types of districts generate conflict, under certain circumstances, and that such conflict may lead to incumbent defeat and superintendent turnover. Further, he suggests that the "rules of the political game" vary with the two types of political cultures, and superintendents would be well advised to take note of these differences and operate accordingly. The important point here is, however, that the dissatisfaction theory operates in both district types. Thus, with the Boyd data, the Minar work is even more supportive of this explanation of local school politics.

Summary

In the final analysis, the public participates—if it wishes and to the extent it is dissatisfied—at the polls. This process of the election of public representatives to govern in the place of the individual and as a substitute for direct participatory democracy is in the best tradition of American representative democracy. It provides the most functional and effective means of democracy yet developed for modern mass society. It works—perhaps in a painfully slow and cumbersome way, but it works!

Under these circumstances the following implications appear to be of critical concern to incumbent school board members and school superintendents.

1. The present structure of policy making in public education is rather impervious to public influence.

Whether superintendents and school boards recognize this or not does not change the fact. *Most* school board members do *not* think of themselves as representatives of the people but rather as trustees for the people. They do *not* vote as the people wish, but as they think best. The noblesse obligé of an elite aristocracy is not in the best tradition of American democracy and not likely to be well accepted by the American public, over time, particularly if the decisions of that "noble group" seems to the public to be wrong.

2. When it seems impossible or at least improbable for the public to influence the present school board and the policy-making process of the local schools, the public will become increasingly aware of school board elections and the possibility of defeating an incumbent while electing another who they believe will better represent them in policy making.

Although reform-type government in education is rather well accepted by the public, it is better accepted by upper-middle- and upper-class constituencies. Perhaps the reason is that those elected to reform-type councils tend to be persons from those constituencies, and their values and subsequent decisions are more akin to upper-middle- and upper-class individuals. In any case, the public will not *perceive* that decisions are in their best interest when it appears to them that their wishes are never heard, their point of view never represented, and their needs never met. The consensual decisions of school boards are likely to appear in this fashion to certain publics. Under these circumstances, influence attempts turn to frustration, frustration to political conflict and action, and finally conflict and action to incumbent defeat.

3. When the superintendent is perceived as part of this elite form of council policy making, the newly elected board member will carry a mandate to fire the present superintendent.

This event has been demonstrated to follow incumbent school board member defeat in a statistically significant number of cases. In such cases the new superintendent will carry a mandate for policy change toward the values of the public that unseated the old incumbent.

As these events and the explanatory process related to them have been reasonably demonstrated by the research reported in this book, board members and superintendents who wish to remain in office should consider developing a normative system that would permit and encourage a more arena and representative council, under certain circumstances. These circumstances include:

1. A school district that is multicultural with groups of people who hold differing values, abilities, needs, and aspirations
2. A school district changed over time because of in-migration or outmigration or economic shifts
3. Increased and/or repeated attempts to influence the present board followed by increased voting patterns against incumbent members

In any case perhaps it is time for school board members to view themselves more in the image of representatives of the people who elect them and the superintendent to be viewed as the administrator who operationalizes the policy enacted by the majority decision of the school board.

Notes

1. Paul D. Blanchard, "Most School Board Members Are Their Own Men (and Women)—Not Conducts of the Public Will," *The American School Board Journal* (May 1974), pp. 47-48.

2. David J. Edgren, "An Analysis of Community Viewpoint on Education and Municipal Governance Issues," unpublished Ph.D. dissertation, Pennsylvania State University, 1976.

3. Frank W. Lutz, "Local School Boards as Sociocultural Systems" in Peter J. Cistone (ed.), *Understanding School Boards* (Lexington, Mass.: Lexington Books, 1975).

4. F.G. Bailey, "Decisions by Consensus in Councils and Committee" in Michael Banton (ed.), *Political Systems and the Distribution of Power* (London: Travislock Publications Limited, 1965).

5. See Audrey Richards and Adam Kuper (eds.), *Councils in Action* (Cambridge, England: The University Press, 1971).

6. Aaron D. Gresson, "External-Internal Mandates and Elite-Arena Behavior in Local School Boards," unpublished Ph.D. dissertation, Pennsylvania State University, 1976.

7. Daniel C. Witmer, "School Board Council Type—Community Diversity and Public Attitude about Schools," unpublished D.Ed. dissertation, Pennsylvania State University, 1976.

8. Dale Mann, *The Politics of Administrative Representation* (Lexington, Mass.: Lexington Books, 1976).

9. David W. Minar, "The Community Basis of Conflict in School System Politics," *American School Board Journal*, vol. 154, no. 3 (March 1967), pp. 33-38.

10. Edward C. Banfield and James Q. Wilson, *City Politics* (Cambridge, Mass.: Harvard University Press, 1963).

11. William L. Boyd, "Community Status and Suburban School Conflict" in Frederick M. Wirt (ed.), *The Policy of the School* (Lexington, Mass.: Lexington Books, 1975).

Council Behavior of School Boards

The research presented thus far and the dissatisfaction theory within which it is grounded rests on three major assumptions:

1. School districts are social-cultural systems comprised of interacting subsystems and are also part of and interact with a larger county, state, and/or national social-cultural system.
2. One of the most important subsystems of a school district is its decision-making, policy-making system—the local school board and the superintendent. It is possible to view this school board decision-making system as a separate sociocultural system within the school district.
3. The school board and the community may exhibit separate and differing values and behaviors; when these become too widely separated (different), conflict will occur.

Based on the above assumptions, it becomes clear that in order to understand, explain, or predict the process of democratic participation within the dissatisfaction theory, one must have some system or model for classifying and understanding the council behavior of the school board. In chapter 2 we briefly set forth the elite-arena council model suggested by Bailey[1] and used by other political anthropologists to study policy councils other than school boards. It is further suggested in chapter 2 that the council type of a school board (elite-arena) interacts with the community type and the structure of the society, producing a predictable level of conflict and enabling one to specify the likelihood of incumbent defeat and superintendent turnover. It was important then to initiate a program of research that would explicitly look at and compare elite and arena school boards and determine how the public, in various communities, evaluated their school boards in relationship to the board's council behavior and compared to other government agencies.

School Boards versus Other Government Agencies

Edgren[2] completed a study of public attitudes and viewpoints regarding education, as contrasted to other municipal issues, and the councils which enacted policy in these areas. A sample of 14 communities in Pennsylvania was selected so as to represent the general community types within the state (excluding the large metropolitan areas), based on size, geographic location, and local tax effort. Data were gathered on the respondents' personal and demographic characteristics, their preference for participation in final decision making in the policy area, and their approval level afforded to various aspects of agencies' (school board or other municipal agencies) decision making. Some 205 respondents were interviewed via telephone while 400 were sampled by self-administered questionnaires. Based on these data, the following statements were statistically confirmed:

1. Citizens who approve of the type of governance afforded by municipal governments also approve of the type of governance provided by their school boards (beyond the .01 level).
2. There is a strong positive association between citizens' expectations for participation in decision making in both municipal and educational areas.
   (a) Citizens are more willing, however, to allow professionals in education rather than professionals in other local governmental areas to make final decisions.
3. The more congruity there is between a citizen's expectations for and perception of participation in and locus of final decision making, the more that citizen approves and is satisfied with the governance of both the school board and other agencies.
4. The more congruity there is between a citizen's expectations for and perception of participation in and locus of decision making, the more that citizen approved of the way the council made decisions and the decisions they made.
   (a) Citizens would reduce the power of the school board as compared to the borough council and would increase the power of educational professionals as compared to municipal civil service professionals.
5. While citizens think school administrators and school boards (in that order) "listen to them," they *do not* think that what they say makes much difference in the decisions of either.
6. Higher SES persons (particularly those whose major income was derived from managerial or professional occupations) were willing to give much more authority to educational administrators than were blue-collar workers. (This may help account for the lower conflict level in high SES districts found by Minar.)

While other discoveries were made in the Edgren study (i.e., parents with more than two children in the family approved more of both school board and borough council action), those stated above have the greatest impact on the dissatisfaction theory presented in this book.

1. There seems to be a political culture that pervades a community and blurs the distinctions between various local types of government and their councils.

2. Regardless of the desired level of participation in decision making, a citizen is more satisfied with the governance council when he/she perceives they are allowed to participate to *that* extent (not more, not less).
3. The generalized citizen is more willing to allow professionals to make educational decisions, thus reducing the power of the school board, as compared to borough councils and civil servants.
   (*a*) The higher SES and the more professional/managerial the occupation of the head of the household, the more this is true.
4. Citizens do not perceive that their opinions make much, if any, difference in the policy decision making of school boards and administrators.

Given this pattern, it is not surprising to find that there is a general acceptance about school issues, that there is more conflict in lower socioeconomic communities, or that the participation (described within the dissatisfaction theory) is episodic and involves incumbent defeat and superintendent turnover.

Elite versus Arena School Boards

It seemed necessary to determine if, in fact, school boards could or did behave in differing council styles (elite-arena) and if so, under what conditions and to what effect. It was decided that the best way to begin would be to first identify two boards that seemed to behave differently under approximately the same time and space conditions and then carefully describe that behavior using ethnographic techniques. Gresson[3] undertook such a study in 1975.

Two school boards in central Pennsylvania were identified that had similar geographic, SES, and enrollment characteristics. One was reputed to be rather open and engaged in public debate, while the other appeared rather closed to public influence and operated by consensus and unanimous vote. Initial observations confirmed these differences, and a 6-month ethnographic study of the school districts was undertaken. Data included participant observation of formal public meetings as well as some "working sessions"; formal interviews of school board members, administrators, and active lay public; informal data gathering (informant interviews); and review of all public records, school board minutes, and selected historic documents about the two school districts. In an unpublished paper[4] these data are summarized and the following analysis of the different council styles provided.

Clearly, district A's board was an elite-type council. There were less than 15 persons on the board. They denied seeking consensus but admitted to discussing things in private, getting the "sense of the board," and not bringing things to a public meeting until everyone agreed about the issue. They "permitted" an occasional nonunanimous vote, as long as it was clear that the issue would pass. They felt they governed for the entire public and rejected the notion of representing factions or constituencies; they held themselves aloof from the people and acted as trustees for them. The superintendent was an important part of the council's decision making. The board admitted to a heavy reliance upon him, and he occasionally took administrative action as a substitute for board action.

District B's board was more nearly an arena board. By state law, it only had nine members; but as the basis for what he thought of as problems and conflict, the superintendent pointed to the fact that it was once much larger and had members who thought of themselves as representatives of separate constituencies. The superintendent was certainly not an integral part of the board decision system at the time of the study. When he attempted to act by "executive action," as a substitute for board action, he found himself in trouble. The board decided many issues by majority, rather than by unanimous vote, and some members expressed their preference for public debate. Certainly, issues were debated publicly. There were factions, and some voting behavior recognized those divisions, although all board members expressed dissatisfaction with that empirical reality and often denied representing a particular faction or area. In spite of these sentiments, the positions taken in public debate indicated "community in council." Both boards acted only in the area of education but broadly within that area, including levying taxes, purchasing, legislating policy, and making decisions on judicial appeal.

The space allocation for the community tended to confirm the community relationship to the boards. For instance, district A set aside only six chairs for the public in an area separate from the board. Board B provided considerably more space for the public and was *surrounded* on two sides by that public.

Based on the above analysis of the ethnographic descriptions of the boards, the application of the elite-arena model used to describe school boards appears useful. Additionally, there is evidence that a culture of school boards exists across the elite-arena range of school boards. Both boards expressed the notion that they were, or ought to be, trustees who act in the interest of a single public and not as individuals representing a particular interest group or constituency; nor did any board members think they should vote as *the public* felt correct. The public, it was generally conceded, did not have the total information or sufficient insight into the problems to know what was best.

In district B, these norms were in conflict with the reality chosen by or imposed upon the board. The conflict between the norms of the school board culture and the political reality of the school board decision-making process caused each board member of the arena board to experience anxiety and frustration. Such statements as "most would prefer a 9-0 vote," "I don't know how to vote anymore," "I'd prefer to be first in the roll call" (or last in another case), "the board would like to trust the superintendent, but he lies" indicated the type of frustration apparent on the arena board.

Conclusions

Based on the above analysis, school boards can be described within the following explanatory model.

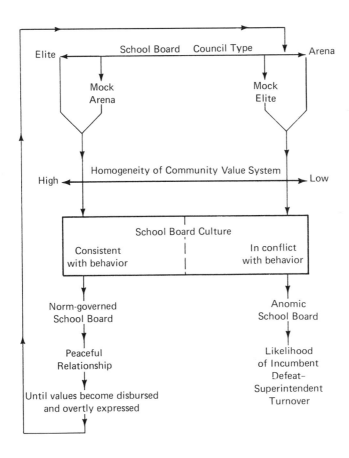

Figure 9-1. Explanatory Model of Elite-Arena School Board Anomie

In figure 9-1, we note that an elite board may occasionally have a nonunanimous vote. As described in the data, this vote will likely be permitted and agreed upon *beforehand*, as long as everyone knows the issue will pass. Thus, this elite board consensus is termed *mock arena* because while it simulates decision by majority vote (and perhaps following some public debate), it is the result of a previous consensus. In like fashion, an arena board may vote unanimously, as board B did, to table the issue of the superintendent's raise. This unanimous vote hides the conflict on the board and momentarily prevents it from erupting into public conflict and hostility. It usually postpones the decision and is merely an agreement to do so. Often the act supports neither position; thus it is not elite but *mock elite*. Council behaviors tend to occur and are more acceptable to the community, as elite behavior occurs in a community with a high degree of homogeneity of community values and arena behavior occurs where there are heterogeneous values and conflict within the community.

These behaviors are perceived by the board themselves and professional school administrators, through their school board culture and the normative structure of that culture. Thus, elite boards are guided by a set of norms accepted by school board members and school administrators. Arena board members find themselves forced to act in ways counter to that normative structure and, believing in the norms provided by the culture, find themselves normless. They do not know how to behave any more. They are in a state of anomie. Individuals in an anomic culture tend to act in "suicidal" ways. In school boards, this may result in involuntary superintendent turnover (supported by our ethnographic data) and is often preceded by incumbent school board member defeat or retirement (supported by data from other studies).

The model also suggests (not supported by data here) that it is likely that an elite board will be forced into arena behavior if community values become sufficiently diverse and overt as they relate to public education.

Council Style and Cultural Congruence

Confident that school boards could and did behave differently in council style and could be classified along a continuum, from more nearly elite to more nearly arena, Witmer[5] undertook a study of 30 selected school boards in Pennsylvania to determine if the relative congruence between community cultural type (from homogeneous to heterogeneous) with the school board council type (from elite to arena) would result in a relationship with the community's evaluation of the school board and the educational program. Data from 825 individual citizens and 214 school board members from these 30 districts were collected from questionnaires mailed to randomly selected citizens in the communities and all school board members in the districts selected. Specific information on the validity and reliability of these questionnaires, the scales inherent in them, and the questionnaires themselves are available in the Witmer dissertation.[6] Community cultural diversity was operationalized by the Lieberson "diversity within populations" formula.[7]

The following findings, statistically significant at or beyond the .05 level, seem relevant to this discussion of the dissatisfaction theory of participation in local school governance.

1. The five school boards that exhibited the highest percentage of nonunanimous voting behavior (at least one standard deviation above the total mean of nonunanimous votes) also exhibited a belief system that was extreme and toward the elite end of board norms. That is, they denied being representatives of factions of the public and thought they should reach consensus and vote unanimously, when in fact they did not.
2. These boards were identified as anomic. That is, they expressed values and

held norms about their "ought to" behavior that did not correspond to, guide, or support the behavior which they empirically exhibited.

3. When the 5 districts identified as anomic were eliminated from the total sample, the remaining 25 districts exhibited the predicted relationship between the congruity of cultural diversity—council behavior and public approval of the school board and the schools. That is, homogeneous districts approved of more elite boards, and heterogeneous districts approved of more arena boards.

4. The general public in all districts desired somewhat more arena-style behavior from their boards than their boards typically exhibited.

Thus, the Witmer study supported statistically many of the grounded assumptions produced by the previous ethnographies. School boards can and do exhibit a variation of council behaviors, from more nearly elite to more nearly arena. The vast majority of them, however, lie nearer the elite end of the continuum than the arena end. Additionally, those in this study that tended most toward the arena end in regard to their voting behavior and public debate expressed norms and values closer to the elite end of the continuum. It seemed that all the boards studied generally rejected the *notion* of individual board members representing segments of the community in the "community in council" fashion suggested by the political anthropologists. Apparently the *vast* majority of school boards are locked into the culture of school boards which requires them to be trustees for all the people—and representatives of none. Further, the more the school board is driven away from behaving in such a fashion (due to conflict), the more strongly they express these norms. Not unlike many exotic cultures, they hold to their myths and beliefs long after these are dysfunctional in terms of operating behavior within the changed environment. They long for the "good old days" and struggle like "The Fiddler on the Roof" to maintain their balance through traditions sealed deep within their culture of school boards. Like Anatevka, it is likely that they will soon be destroyed. They are an anomic society. Either they are normless, or they hold norms that do not sanction, govern, guide, or support the behaviors they find it impossible not to exhibit. Conflict will escalate, incumbents will be defeated, there will be superintendent turnover, and finally a new state of equilibrium will be achieved and a period of peace and stability will return—not through belief in the traditional (in cargo-cult fashion) but through the democratic political process of public participation, described by the dissatisfaction theory of local school governance.

How Do We Know

Statisticians are fond of reciting the level of significance with which they have demonstrated "their truth." "I have found a difference," they confidently state.

Educational practitioners, often with a smile on their faces, are fond of telling the researchers, "But it doesn't make any difference!" Too often both are correct! Essentially what we need to know is what can or does or could happen in educational organizations, not only what has been demonstrated to have a significant statistical relationship but also what actually offers a hope of producing an operational change (a difference) in the educational process.

Suppose one demonstrated, at a statistical significance of .01, that children who learned to read from texts printed on blue paper achieved more at the end of first grade (on standard reading tests) than children learning to read from the standard white-paper texts. Suppose the researcher had correlated shades of blue (scaled 1 to 10, with white being 1) and found a positive correlation of .016 between reading scores and increasing the tint of blue paper in the texts. Further, suppose that there were 2000 randomly selected first-graders in the research sample. This finding is significant at the .01 level, but the correlation accounts for less than one-thousandth of 1 percent of the variance in the reading scores of those 2000 pupils. In other words, "The difference doesn't make any difference!"

Much of what has been said here is supported by statistical research significant at levels generally acceptable in educational research. But does it make any difference? Incumbent defeat follows change in certain socioeconomic-political indicators in the district and certain types of school board tax response, at an acceptable level of significance. Incumbent defeat is followed by superintendent turnover at the .01 level of significance. But does all this make any difference? Put another way, do these events happen in such a way so as to produce a political policy change in local school districts? Is it real, in addition to being statistically significant?

To answer this question, we may return to the ethnographic studies reported above (i.e., the Iannaccone-Lutz study[8] and the Gresson study[9]). But this evidence can be faulted because in the former study the researchers already had incumbent defeat and were trying to explain the process and its result, and in the latter case the districts were selected because the researcher wanted to study specific types of school boards and so set out to describe them. The question still remains for the skeptic: Do these events happen in the "natural world"? Would one run into this series of events even when looking for something else? The following would seem to provide a rather substantial "yes" to those questions.

Chuchura[10] attempted to study a school district embroiled in serious labor relations conflict, to determine if the model, described in the private industrial sector by Whyte[11] in *Pattern for Industrial Peace*, might account for the emergence of a new level of accommodation in the public school sector, in similar fashion as it did in the private industrial sector. Chuchura did not set out to find, nor did anything Whyte described suggest, the political change and the events described in the dissatisfaction theory. As it turned out, however, the following series of events occurred within the case study that parallels exactly the dissatisfaction theory:

1. There was a long period of tranquility prior to the conflict (no incumbent defeat, no superintendent turnover).
2. As conflict arose, because of certain changes in the district and the employer-employee-community relations, incumbent defeat followed incumbent defeat three times and each time that defeat was followed by superintendent turnover.
3. Finally a successor superintendent, with the support of a new majority on the school board, initiated a number of policy changes in the district that were more in line with the new values expressed by the teachers and the community.
4. That policy shift has (for the moment at least) ushered in a new area of stability and tranquility in employee relations as well as school board-community relations.

Based on such evidence, supplementing the research previously reported in this book, we feel confident in stating that these differences do make a difference. *The dissatisfaction theory of public participation in local school policy describes a process that not only is significant at appropriate statistical levels but really occurs and does make a difference in the processes of educational organizations. It is practical!*

Notes

1. F.G. Bailey, "Decisions by Consensus in Councils and Committees" in Michael Banton (ed.), *Political Systems and the Distribution of Power* (London: Tavistock Publications Limited, 1965).

2. David J. Edgren, "An Analysis of Community Viewpoint on Education and Municipal Issues," unpublished doctoral dissertation, Pennsylvania State University, 1976.

3. Arron D. Gresson, "External-Internal Mandates and Elite-Arena Behavior of Local School Boards," unpublished doctoral dissertation, Pennsylvania State University, 1976.

4. Frank W. Lutz and Arron Gresson, "Anomie in Local School Board Council Behavior," unpublished paper presented at the American Anthropological Association, 1976.

5. Daniel C. Witmer, "School Board Council Type—Community Diversity and Public Attitude about Schools," unpublished doctoral dissertation, Pennsylvania State University, 1976.

6. Ibid.

7. Stanley Lieberson, "Measuring Population Diversity" *American Sociological Review*, vol. 34 (December 1969), pp. 850-62.

8. Laurence Iannaccone and Frank W. Lutz, *Politics, Power and Policy: Governing Local School Districts* (Columbus, Ohio: Charles E. Merrill Publishing Company, 1970).

9. Gresson, "External-Internal Mandates."

10. Andrew Chuchura, "Change from Strife to Accommodation in Organizational Behavior as Effected by Collective Bargaining: A Case Study," unpublished doctoral dissertation, Pennsylvania State University, 1977.

11. William Foote Whyte, *Pattern for Industrial Peace* (New York: Harper and Brothers Publisher, 1951).

10 The Dissatisfaction Theory of Governance: Implications for Practice and Research

Introduction

Two questions, sometimes carelessly mixed, have dominated the study of local school government in the United States during this century: Who governs? and Is it democratic?[1] George Counts sought to answer both simultaneously by examining the social composition of school boards produced by the municipal reform.[2] His work has been followed in numerous studies with the same findings. The general inferences drawn were that school district government was less than democratic and that the upper middle class governed it.

The early 1950s saw the first major turning point in our understanding of school boards and local school district government. Charters summarized the findings to that point[3] and in a short but trenchant statement criticized the limitations of such inferences and called upon researchers to ask more sophisticated questions.[4] Research of increasing sophistication developed on board member roles during that decade but generally still failed to go beyond the survey or single interview as data-collecting tools.[5] The social class composition of boards and the superintendent's self-report on who governed were taken as gospel in these studies.[6]

A major change in the attention given to the politics of education by scholars from educational administration and by political scientists can be seen at the end of the 1950s and during the first half of the next decade. The call by Thomas H. Eliot in 1959 for a better understanding of educational politics[7] is often mistakenly seen as a turning point in that understanding. It was preceded by a similar call the previous year by Wallace Sayre.[8] However, the development of a research subfield, the politics of education, subsequent to these pleas of political scientists and the earlier call by Charters, was not produced by these pleas. Instead it reflects more the pragmatic political realities of the challenges to the ideology of the municipal reform, especially the political myth of authority within which public and school administration are embedded.[9] Eliot's 1959 call is, however, a useful benchmark from which to view the subsequent theoretical development about local school government.

As late as 1959 our tested knowledge of the political realities of local school government carried us only a little beyond the constitutional understanding of a civics textbook. Eliot emphasized the fact that since schools are the objects of local control through elected school boards, they could hardly be considered apolitical.[10] In noting the significant influence of a few graduate schools upon that profession, he foreshadowed the major conclusion of the next decade of research, as did the more precise but narrower statement by Sayre in 1958.[11] That conclusion is that if one insists upon a single label response to the question "Who governs?" in public education, then the research suggests that the answer is "organized school employee elites."[12] While that is not the most useful way to ask the question, it is easy to understand why that general formulation of the central question dominated much of the last decade's research. In 1962, commenting on his group's research strategy of centering upon the state as the unit for analysis, Eliot wrote, "There are tens of thousands of districts and in each the political pattern is different."[13] Apart from considerations of research strategy, this statement, as it was written by an earlier leader in the study of the politics of education, reveals the theoretical bankruptcy of our scientific understanding of local school government only 15 years ago. This conclusion is further supported by Eliot's own: "To formulate and test a general theory of school district politics would demand the examination of an impracticably large number of districts."[14] Today that statement is no longer tenable as the evidence of over a decade of theoretically guided research reported in this book alone attests. In addition, there exist other bodies of theoretically guided research which also address the questions "Who governs?" and "Is it democratic?"[15] When an emerging area of inquiry displays opposing theoretical positions supported by empirical work done in pursuit of those theoretical positions, it begins to have something meaningful to say about future research strategy and offers alternative guides to practitioners.

Three Schools of Thought

Before discussing the differences among three approaches,[16] each seemingly a thoughtful analysis based upon solid research, it may be well to note some of their points of agreement.[17] (1) All three are concerned with the basic questions of control of local school district policy and operations. (2) They share with some variation the judgment that the key actors deserving attention are the district's citizens, the board, and school administrators. This implies that it is the interaction among these three sorts of actors which, when properly examined, will answer the question of whether the local school district is a democratic government. (3) Above all they are interested in the issue of whether the local school district is democratic. However, as one examines how each school of thought states what it considers the relevant aspects of that interaction among these actors, their divergence begins to be seen. That divergence becomes wider as issues of research method used by each are comparatively examined. These theories come into greatest conflict as they turn to the bottom-line question, "Is the local school district a democratic government?" At that point it becomes clear that each research camp is using a different criterion for democratic government because of their respective central definitions of democracy, i.e., participation, representation, or dissatisfaction. Three conceptualizations of Local Education Agency (LEA) molding and becoming shaped by research on local school district politics of the last 15 years may be thought of as (1) a continuous competition theory, (2) a decision output theory, and (3) a dissatisfaction theory. Each of these conceptualizations may be discerned as respectively predominating in the writing of particular researchers which severely reflect the influence of distinct schools of Western democratic political thought (although the politics of education researchers so influenced often do not indicate awareness of that influence).

In brief, the continuous competition theory reflects a primary concern with citizen participation, especially the amount of it and group bias reflected in it within educational governments. Decision output theory is primarily concerned with the responsiveness called *representation* of the political system of education to public needs or demands, although which is not always clear. Dissatisfaction theory is essentially interested in the processes by which public dissatisfaction with local educational governments leads to traumatic episodic change in it. Each school additionally shares a concern for the central issues of the other two and uses aspects of their major concept but subordinates these to its own major concept. Thus dissatisfaction theory cares about the responsiveness of LEA politics to the public's needs and demands. It is also concerned with participation—both the degree and the group bias in it—especially as these change over time. These are, however, subordinated in dissatisfaction theory to a central concern for the capacity of that dissatisfaction to redirect local school government through changes in participating groups and for how these changes reflect public demand and meet public needs. Similarly each of the other two theories uses concepts of dissatisfaction and adjustment within their explanations of local school politics without giving these ideas predominance in their theories. So one could readily develop a taxonomy of key theoretical concepts interconnecting these three schools of thought.

Continuous Universal Competition Theory

The most popular theory in local school district politics stresses the resolution of conflict, what Banfield and Wilson distinguished from the public service function of government as its political one.[18] The work of David Minar[19] and more recently that of Harmon Zeigler and Kent Jennings[20] rely upon a continuous competition theory of democratic politics to guide their research questions and methods. The central assumptions are a mix of normative and scientific political theory. Its scientific aspect is a variant of group interest theory while its normative premises express a belief in maximum egalitarian participation. Its interest group strand reflects the recent work of David Truman's *The Govern-*

mental Process,[21] which was modeled on and shaped largely by Bentley's *The Process of Government.*[22] Indeed Zeigler describes his theory as derived from Bentley with the reintroduction of the psychological dimension,[23] which Bentley had rejected and systematically detached from his theoretical position. Its earlier theoretical antecedents may be found in James Harrington's *Oceana.* The normative premises of the theory reflect the general belief that democracy is especially concerned with universal citizen participation. In this aspect its debt to the tradition of Locke and even more to Rousseau may be seen.

The combination of interest group theory assumptions and normative premises about broad participation leads to the essential criterion position that democracy requires the regular, continuous political competition and opposition among a wide range of informed groups with diverse interests in policy decisions. Hence the key research questions guided by this theory lie in the conflict resolution domain of government functions rather than in its service functions.[24] They are directed toward issues of (1) the universality of participation and continuity of competition among interests for school board election, (2) representativeness of school board member points of view on issues as responding to citizen interests within their districts, and (3) the transmission of these through the relations between boards and superintendents to policy decisions. Similarly, attention is directed to school-community conflict, which is viewed as produced primarily by variations in social class characteristics and the heterogeneity of district populations.[25] Given the normative premises of this school and the finding of relatively small active voting proportions of citizens and infrequent local district conflict described by Martin as episodic,[26] these researchers' interpretations of the significance of issues are reasonable. They see the board's true function as legitimating policies of the school's professional elite to the community rather than injecting community interests into these.[27] Low voter turnout, frequent reelection of board incumbents, and episodic rather than continuous political conflict are viewed as evidence of structural, ideological, and political resource limitations upon an open interplay of competitive interests.

So this school of thought has concluded that our present school district governments are fundamentally and perhaps unredeemably undemocratic because, in the words of one of its leading spokesman, "... school boards are likely to become spokesmen for the superintendent to the community; their representational roles are reversed, and the superintendent becomes the dominant policy maker."[28]

Decision Output Theory

Others seek to explain the local district's politics by using the delivery of its public service, its other government function, as their point of departure rather than its conflict-resolution function. In contrast to the continuous competition criterion of the first theory, this theory uses the correspondence between the school system's response to either citizen demands or client needs. When they emphasize demands, they tend to focus on administrative decisions and the results of these for their comparison. Instead of placing stress upon citizen needs, this theoretical school moves toward a normative theory using primarily egalitarian criteria to judge democracy with touches reminiscent of Rousseau's general will. Both the more scientific and the more normative subgroups of the school are indebted, often unawares, to public administration theory for their language and general conceptual frame of reference.

The point of view may be seen in the work of Frederick M. Wirt, Michael W. Kirst, and Joel S. Berke.[29],[30] Their characteristic concern is with the product of political and administrative decisions—system outputs and their outcomes— rather than the system's processes whether these products are desegregation, curriculum, or finance.[31] In that concern they approach an old, naively empirical, and atheoretical educational administration finance tradition which at last peaked in the work of H. Thomas James.[32] The newer political studies instead reflect the work of David Easton in political science.[33] His model is the heuristic device used especially by Wirt to shape the presentation of much politics of education research.[34] The debt owed by this conceptual approach to management or administrative theory is clear in its use of Easton's model, the language used (e.g., input, output and feedback), and the older educational finance tradition. This relationship may be inevitable in a theory which takes a product rather than process as a point of departure since that conceptualization reflects the market environment of the industrial world in which its parent political ideology was born.

Commenting on the rise of the self-conscious study of public administration, Dwight Waldo says, "public administration as a literature and a body of concepts also come to contain a new theory or philosophy of government."[35] This philosophy is the doctrine of the administrative state, "a reinterpretation of the meaning democracy for . . . the new, urban America."[36] It owes much to scientific management orientations and is embodied in the tenets of the municipal reform. Whether emphasizing centralization, bureaucracy and efficiency, accountability and finance, or egalitarian education outputs, the product emphasis on responsiveness is inevitably drawn to an administrative focus for its research. One recent development of this product orientation in the writing of William Boyd indicates this drift. Concerned for the responsiveness of the system (viewed as its delivery of services), he writes, "The view of what is proper in board-staff relationships has so permeated thinking on the subject that most writing and research on the topic until the contemporary critique—and a good deal even now—has focused far more on the *process* than on the *product* of the relationships."[37] Boyd's understanding that his emphasis is a product of shifting administrative doctrines is clearly pointed out by him.[38] He uses Kaufman's simplified description of changes in public administration doctrines as his conceptual frame of reference.[39] The fundamental problem with his conceptualization of the problem is articulated in his conclusion that we are doomed to effective representation because "this is the price of the simultaneous pursuit of democracy and efficiency."[40] This may, indeed, be true; but if so, it is only true as long as the new doctrine of efficiency is held of equal value with that of democracy.

The most recent step in the extension of this political theory in the politics of education literature reveals even more its sometimes obscured basic bias as an apologia for administrator power through the development of a new definition of representation. Rather than take its old meaning of the redefinition of an individual's character through presenting him a second time in a public character via electoral structures which redefine that citizen,[41] the emphasis of language from this school follows Hannah Pitkin's substantive representation concept, which is a normative theory of democracy. It is "acting in the interest of the represented" which makes for democracy.[42] The correspondence between what officials do and what their constituents or clients would have them do or need is the key criterion value for judging the democratic character of local school politics. So Kirst based his judgment on a combination of Easton's policy outcome concepts (for his theory base) and Pitkin's political philosophy (for his normative criterion), concluding that the local district was undemocratic.[43]

Dale Mann carries the normative definition of democracy as substantive representation responding to client wishes for public service to what is, for now, its logical extreme. Political representation, he defines, as ". . . the way school administrators take account of the needs and interests of the public," and as "the proper inclusion and weighing of community wishes and interests in administrative action."[44] His data come from research on the "representational" role orientations of school administrators, which he organizes following Pitkin by using her substantive representation definition under the headings of trustee, delegate, and politico types of administrators.[45] The trustee considers himself responsible rather than responsive, and the delegate is the converse of that, with the politico shuttling between the delegate and trustee stances. It is easy to reject this use of language and concepts which makes administrator attitudes the test of democracy. If the results of the New York City selection and socialization processes for building principals become the critical test for democracy,[46] then the language of political science in the 1970s has become the sociological jargon of the 1930s. Much more significant is the fact that product-based political theories tend to make the dependent variable of outcome the critical test of democracy. In so doing, theory tends to lose its scientific character, its capacity to systematically explain, however accurate its descriptions may be. Its judgmental start is its finish. Research comes dangerously close to a forensic rather than explanatory character in this way. Practical advice becomes hortatory evangelism characterized as training in educational administration through most of this century. Normative premises substitute for causal paths. However, this body of research splendidly footnotes the basic public administration theory and administration apologia for power found at its roots.

Methodologically both continuous competition and decision output theories can settle for and characteristically use cross-sectional rather than longitudinal data-collecting research designs. These are seriously defective for scientific purposes. They make the distinction between independent and dependent variables empirically untestable. The declaration of which are the independent and which are the dependent variables can be switched at will by changing their positions on computer cards. This defect is less important if the research goal is to enter a judgment about the system's democratic character rather than the discovery of cause-and-effect relations. This is particularly true when the criteria variable is operationalized as amount of participation, as by Zeigler and his colleagues,[47] or as representation operationalized as the administrator's own role expectations, as by Mann.[48] Research descriptively reporting data on these indicators can enter a judgment as to the democratic character of local school district politics without the need for scientific understanding and hypothesis testing.

Despite their methodological similarities, these schools differ to some extent in their judgments of local school districts as democratic governments. Zeigler and Jennings declare them undemocratic because administrators control boards and conclude that local boards "should govern or be abolished."[49] Those scholars using decision output concepts derived from Easton tend to agree. Instead, Mann (and even more Boyd), judging the democratic character of local educational politics, enters a verdict which is less sure. For them the answer is "it depends." Specifically it depends on whether the administrator administers in the interest of the client or not. In any case these writers appear to reject the basic tension between administration and representation which is central and needed in the continuous competition review. Dissatisfaction theory instead leads to a firm "yes" answer to the question as to whether there is democracy in school district governance.

Dissatisfaction Theory

From the viewpoint of dissatisfaction theory, continuous competition and decision output theories appear to present us with a Hobson's choice. Their respective central concepts of participation and substantive representation doom the local school district to disappearance as a democratic governmental unit, the one by calling for an empirically nonexistent category of nearly universal participation, the other by subjecting us to an old tyranny, for administrator representation is despotism writ small. The political myth of universal partici-pation has always stood in the way of understanding how democratic societies such as in England and the United States work. The essential feature of a free people is freedom, not involvement.[50] The delivery of services people want or which are "best" for them may be the fruit of benevolent despotism as much as of any other political system.

Dissatisfaction theory explains the local school district politics by beginning with the recognition that the political myth of regular widespread participation in self-government is unrealistic and unsupported by empirical evidence in any representative or democratic society on which we have data, from Athens to date. Thus the theory follows the line hewn by Mosca in his theory of the political class, as acknowledged by Iannaccone and Lutz in their earlier work.[51] Central to the theory is Michel's "Iron Law of Oligarchy." Premises of dissatisfaction theory are the inevitable drift toward an organized central elite in *all* political systems and the tendency of that elite to perpetuate itself. As a result, over time political systems tend to become increasingly closed to citizens' demands. At the same time as these tendencies toward choosing the governmental dimension of a society continue their natural processes toward increased stability, perpetuation of the elite, and continuance of the same political ideology and related program values in schools, the larger essentially nonpolitical citizenry changes as a result of a variety of factors (e.g., demographic mobility, generational transitions, and educationally altered expectations).[52] Thus two dimensions—the governmental one occupied by political people and the societal one largely composed of civic people—may be seen as characterizing any community including the school district.[53] As the first statement of dissatisfaction theory in the literature of the politics of education pointed out, these two parts of the community are closely related to each other and they are interdependent.[54] Given the natural tendency toward centralizing, closedness and stabilizing in governments, and drift toward change in the larger society, a widening gap between the political elite in power and the others is likely to be created. Then we will find the voters voting to bring the government into line with the larger society's wishes.[55] Hence this school of thought in the politics of education is interested in studying the developmental process of citizen *dissatisfaction* with the local school's programs and the establishment and discovery of countervailing power to offset the inevitable government by a few. Therefore dissatisfaction theory identifies democratic control with episodic adjustment of school district policy to the will or values of the larger community, rather than with any minimum level of continuous competition or correspondence in administrative decisions to client needs.

The search for an explanation of the process of adjustment between policy making and the larger community focuses on a chain of events by which dissatisfaction (due to either the exhaustion of citizen satisfaction with a previous policy mandate or changes in citizen expectations and demands for educational programs) leads to traumatic political change and the subsequent adaptation of the school organization. The theory is more influenced by a concern for explanation than by its normative aspect. Thus, for example, Iannaccone and Lutz and their students have focused their research on longitudinal studies. These include evidence of community changed dissatisfaction (DIS) reflected in voting behavior leading next to incumbent school board member defeat (ID) followed within 2 years by involuntary superintendent turnover (STO) and outside succession (OS). That line of theory (DIS/ID/STO/OS) is now well established in over a decade of research across the United States. These findings constitute the empirical basis for their conclusion, in sharp contrast to other scholarly schools in the politics of education. In reference to the first set of verificational studies testing the line of DIS/ID/STO/OS, Iannaccone wrote, "in no way do the findings of these studies justify the conclusion that the local district 'must go' because it cannot or does not change educationally to meet its citizen demands. . . . Despite the delay imposed by the resistance of the professionals . . . one must suspect that the public does get the educational changes it wants."[56] Now ten years of additional research, replicating and refining that earlier work, has greatly strengthened the evidence for that conclusion. Democracy *is* at work in the present local school district! Whether university professors and federal bureaucrats like what people decide at the local level or not, that local government is altered by systematic—not random episodic—political change.

Less normative than continuous competition and decision output theory, it too is partially a normative theory of democracy. Liberty of opposition seen in the capacity to unseat those in office is the normative aspect of dissatisfaction theory despite its basic scientific character. It is liberty and especially the existence of a public opposition to the governing elite which are viewed by this school of thought as the only effective check on those who hold office, elected and appointive. That criterion of democracy goes back at least to Machiavelli and is reflected in Peter Bachrach.[57]

As Lutz has pointed out elsewhere,

. . . because interests and values differ in a society, because resources are always limited, and because political decisions benefit one group's values and interests, those decisions must also disadvantage others. Lord Acton is reported to have said, "Power corrupts and absolute power corrupts absolutely." The critical question then may not be, "Who governs?" but "Who has access to modify the governance, under what conditions, and how?" If there is a tendency to the "Iron Law of Oligarchy," if "power corrupts and absolute power corrupts absolutely," and if those who exercise power sooner or later do so in their own best interest, then the only political difference in governance systems is whether the power is absolute or whether, when other interests are sufficiently unattended, those others can alter the governance system and by what means.[58]

Given this normative criterion, the research of more than 15 years in local school political changes, guided by dissatisfaction theory and in turn developing its application to LEA politics, renders an uncompromising conclusion. As far as the evidence goes, whatever the room for improvement, the American school district is fundamentally a successful democratic government. Thus the most important practical implication is to strengthen the local school district.

Questions on how to improve the episodic changes resulting from civic dissatisfaction and how to make it less traumatic and speed its completion lead to implications about fundamental missing links in the research chain between citizen dissatisfaction and school delivery service adjustment to this dissatisfaction. Until two other aspects of the theory's predictve system are tested, its claims to explain the adjustment of the school's public service function to citizen demands by means of the local district's political function of conflict resolution through local board elections remain plausible but unproved. The conclusions are that (1) there is a lack of adequate longitudinal studies testing the episodic stages of dissatisfaction and incumbent defeat, followed by citizen satisfaction and incumbent reelection, and then again followed by a new stage of incumbent defeat, and (2) research is needed also to longitudinally test the presently hypothesized school organizational adaptations. Treating drastic change in the political life of the school district as the independent variable and systematically investigating subsequent organizational changes as the dependent variables will provide a necessary step in complete testing of dissatisfaction theory. That crucial work is missing. Not only does it represent a necessary test to complete the judgment on the democratic nature of the present school district community's capacity to adjust the system to its demands; but also it is needed to link our knowledge of political change in local districts to learning outcomes. However, despite these present lacunae in our knowledge, even after years of loss of discretionary power to Washington and to state capitols the evidence indicates that the local school district and the local board continue as the primary grass-roots unit of democratic government in America. This is true even when viewed not through a civics textbook but through the most scientific and least normative theory and research approach in the politics of education. Defending its continued existence as well as improving its democratic structures and processes may be a most significant battlefield in the perennial struggle to keep a free society.

Notes

1. For the recent period of research see Laurence Iannaccone and Peter J. Cistone, *The Politics of Education* (Eugene, Ore.: University of Oregon, Eric Clearinghouse on Educational Management, 1974).

2. George S. Counts, *The Social Composition of Boards of Education* (Chicago: University of Chicago Press, 1927).

3. W.W. Charters, Jr., "Social Class Analysis and the Control of Public Education," *Harvard Educational Review*, vol. 23, no. 4 (Fall 1953), pp. 268-82.

4. W.W. Charters, Jr., "Beyond the Survey in School Board Research," *Educational Administration and Supervision*, vol. 41 (December 1955), pp. 449-52.

5. See, for example, Maurice E. Stapley, *Effective School Board Membership* (Chicago: Midwest Administration Center, University of Chicago, 1952).

6. Note the data base of even the most sophisticated of these: Neal Gross, Ward S. Mason, and Alexander W. McEachern, *Explorations in Role Analysis: Studies of the School Superintendency Role* (New York: John Wiley & Sons, 1958).

7. Thomas H. Eliot, "Toward an Understanding of Public School Politics," *American Political Science Review*, vol. 53 (1959), pp. 1032-51.

8. Note the penetrating insight into future findings displayed in Wallace S. Sayre, "Additional Observations on the Study of Administration," *Teachers College Record*, vol. 60, no. 2 (November 1958), pp. 73-76.

9. Laurence Iannaccone, "Three Views of Change in Educational Politics," in Jay D. Sinbner (ed.), *The Politics of Education*, 76th Yearbook, part II of the National Society for the Study of Education (Chicago: University of Chicago Press, 1977), pp. 255-86.

10. Eliot, "Toward an Understanding."

11. Sayre, "Additional Observations."

12. Laurence Iannaccone and Peter J. Cistone, *The Politics of Education* (Eugene, Ore.: Eric Clearinghouse on Educational Management, University of Oregon, 1974), p. 65 *et passim*.

13. Nicholas A. Masters, Robert H. Salisbury, and Thomas H. Eliot, *State Politics and the Public Schools* (New York: Alfred A. Knopf, 1964), p. v.

14. Ibid.

15. One of these may be seen especially in L. Harmon Zeigler and M. Kent Jennings with G. Wayne Peak, *Governing American Schools: Political Interaction in Local School Districts* (North Scituate, Mass.: Duxbury Press, 1974). The other may be seen in William L. Boyd, "School Board Administrative Staff Relationships" in Peter J. Cistone (ed.), *Understanding School Boards* (Lexington, Mass.: D.C. Heath and Company, 1975), pp. 103-129 and Dale Mann, *The Politics of Administrative Representation* (Lexington, Mass.: D.C. Heath and Company, 1976).

16. In fact, one may discern at least four schools of thought in the research literature on the LEA politics of education. In addition to the three discussed below, the work influenced by Counts, *Social Composition of Boards of Education*, and the dominant view in researchers following Floyd Hunter, *Community Power Structure* (Chapel Hill: University of North Carolina Press, 1953), use a theory of economic determinism through their stratified social class model as their explanatory theory. Ralph Kimbrough, *Political Power and Educational Decision Making* (Chicago: Rand McNally and Company, 1964), provides the best-known example of this older school in modern politics of education work.

17. This analysis is indebted to an early unpublished paper, Douglas E. Mitchell, "School District Politics and Democratic Theory: The Need for New Research," Riverside, Calif.: Mimeographed, 1976.

18. Edward C. Banfield and James Q. Wilson, *City Politics* (Cambridge, Mass.: Harvard University Press, 1963).

19. David W. Minar, "The Community Basis of Conflict in School System Politics," *American Sociological Review*, vol. 31, no. 6 (December 1966).

20. Zeigler and Jennings with G. Wayne Peak, *Governing American Schools.*

21. David B. Truman, *The Governmental Process* (New York: Knopf, 1951).

22. Arthur Bentley, *The Process of Government* (San Antonio, Tex.: Principia Press of Trinity University, 1949).

23. L. Harmon Zeigler and G. Wayne Peak, *Interest Groups in American Society*, 2d ed. (Englewood Cliffs, N.J.: Prentice-Hall, Inc., 1972), pp. 8-11.

24. This distinction follows Banfield and Wilson, *City Politics.*

25. See especially Minar, "The Community Basis of Conflict," and David W. Minar, *Educational Decision-Making in Suburban Communities*, Cooperative Research Project #2440 O.E. of U.S.H.W., 1966.

26. Roscoe C. Martin, *Government and the Suburban School* (Syracuse, N.Y.: Syracuse University Press, 1962).

27. See for another example Norman D. Kerr, "The School Board as an Agency of Legitimation," *Sociology of Education*, vol. 38 (Fall 1964), pp. 34-59.

28. Zeigler and Jennings with Peak, *Governing American Schools*, p. 92.

29. Frederick M. Wirt and Michael W. Kirst, *The Political Web of American Schools* (Boston: Little, Brown and Co., 1972).

30. Joel S. Berke et al., "Federal Aid to Public Education, Who Benefits?" in Joel S. Berke and Michael W. Kirst (eds.), *Federal Aid to Education* (Lexington, Mass.: D.C. Heath and Co., 1972).

31. Even the process most central to this writing focuses upon the feedback product rather than internal modulation aspects of the political systems model they use; see Wirt and Kirst, *The Political Web.*

32. H. Thomas James et al., *Determinants of Educational Expenditures in Large Cities of the United States* (Stanford, Calif.: School of Education, Stanford University, 1966).

33. David Easton, *The Political System* (New York: Alfred A. Knopf, 1953).

34. Frederick M. Wirt, "Theory and Research Needs in the Study of American Educational Politics," *Journal of Educational Administration* vol. 8, no. 1 (May 1970), pp. 53-70, and his chapter "American Schools as a Political System: A Bibliographic Essay" in Michael W. Kirst (ed.), *State, School and Politics* (Lexington, Mass.: D.C. Heath and Co., 1972).

35. Dwight Waldo, *The Study of Public Administration* (New York: Random House, 1955), p. 19.

36. Ibid.

37. Boyd, "School Board Administrative Staff Relationships," p. 109.

38. Ibid., p. 105.

39. Herbert Kaufman, "Emerging Conflicts in the Doctrines of Public Administration," *American Political Science Review*, vol. 50, no. 4 (December 1956), pp. 1057-73.

40. Ibid., p. 126.

41. In contrast see Laurence Iannaccone and David K. Wiles, "The Changing Politics of Urban Education," *Education and Urban Society*, vol. 3, no. 3 (May 1971), pp. 255-64.

42. Hannah F. Pitkin, *The Concept of Representation* (Berkeley: University of California Press, 1967) quoted in Dale Mann, *The Politics of Administrative Representation* (Lexington, Mass.: D.C. Heath and Co., 1976), p. 11.

43. Michael W. Kirst, *The Politics of Education at the Local, State, and Federal Levels* (Berkeley, Calif.: McCutchan Publishing Co., 1970), p. 11.

44. Dale Mann, "School Administrators as Political Representatives" in Frederick M. Wirt (ed.), *The Polity of the School* (Lexington, Mass.: D.C. Heath and Company, 1975), p. 85.

45. Ibid.; Mann, *The Politics of Administrative Representation.*

46. See Laurence Iannaccone, *Politics in Education* (New York: The Center for Applied Research in Education, Inc., 1977), pp. 25-26.

47. Zeigler and Jennings with Peak, *Governing American Schools.*

48. Mann, *The Politics of Administrative Representation.*

49. Zeigler and Jennings with Peak, *Governing American Schools*, p. 254.

50. Ernest Barker, *Reflections on Government* (London: Oxford University Press, 1942).

51. Laurence Iannaccone and Frank W. Lutz, *Politics, Power and Policy: The Governing of Local School Districts* (Columbus, Ohio: Charles E. Merrill Publishing Co., 1970), p. 46.

52. Iannaccone, *Politics in Education*, pp. 4-18.

53. The distinction here follows the "Homo Politico" and "Homo Civicus" one used by Robert A. Dahl, *Who Governs?* (New Haven: Yale University Press, 1961).

54. Iannaccone, *Politics in Education*, p. 16.

55. Ibid., p. 17.

56. Ibid., pp. 98-100.

57. Peter Bachrach, *The Theory of Democratic Elitism: A Critique* (Boston: Little, Brown and Company, 1967).

58. Frank W. Lutz, "Methods and Conceptualizations of Political Power in Education" in *The Politics of Education: Seventy-sixth Yearbook of the National Society for the Study of Education* (Chicago: University of Chicago Press, 1977), p. 32.

List of Contributors

Margaret A. Ramsey received the Ph.D. from the University of New Mexico. She has been on the faculty of The Pennsylvania State University and served as special assistant to the Secretary of Education in Massachusetts.

John Walden received the Ph.D. from Claremont Graduate School and is presently professor and department chairman of Educational Administration at Auburn University.

Allen W. Moen received the Ph.D. from The Pennsylvania State University, has served in several administrative roles in public education. He is presently superintendent of the Independent School District #883, Rockford, Minnesota.

Martin Burlingame received the Ph.D. from University of Chicago. He was on the faculty of University of New Mexico and is now professor of Educational Administration at the University of Illinois, Urbana.

William L. Garberina Sr. received the Ph.D. from The Pennsylvania State University and has served in several administrative positions in public education, presently as principal in the Philadelphia Public Schools.

Douglas E. Mitchell received the Ph.D. from Claremont Graduate School. He is now on the faculty of the University of California, at Riverside.

About the Editors

Frank W. Lutz is professor of education and associate in the Center of Higher Education at The Pennsylvania State University where he directed the Division of Education Policy Studies from 1968-1973. He has formally been a member of the faculties of New York University and Washington University and has served as research director for the State of New Mexico.

From 1960-1963, Dr. Lutz was an elected member of a local school board in St. Louis County, Missouri. He presently serves on the national board of Opportunities Academy for Management Training. He has authored, edited or co-authored five books and numerous articles and chapters in the field of the politics and anthropology of education.

Dr. Lutz received the B.S., M.S. and Ed.D from Washington University (St. Louis).

Laurence Iannaccone is acting associate dean and department chairperson of the Graduate School of Education at the University of California at Santa Barbara and is program leader in educational administration. Mr. Iannaccone has been on the faculties of the Ontario Institute for Studies in Education and the University of Toronto Educational Theory Department, Harvard, The Claremont Graduate School, Washington University and New York University.

Mr. Iannaccone has served as a member of the Advisory Board of the Educational Policy Research Center at Syracuse and as a consultant to the federally supported Experimental Schools Program. He is presently a member of the National Institute for Education's Task Force on Educational Governance and Organization. *Politics in Education*, (Prentice Hall, 1967), and *Politics, Power and Policy: The Governing of Local School Districts* with Frank Lutz, (Charles Merrill Publishing Company, 1970), are titles representative of his continuing research interest. His most recent publication is a 1974 monograph, with Peter Cistone, developed for the ERIC Clearing House on Education Management, *The Politics of Education*.

Mr. Iannaccone is currently chairperson of the Government and Professional Liaison Advisory Committee of the American Educational Research Association. As well, he is editor of the *Review of Educational Research*.

He earned the B.A. and M.A. degrees in government at the University of Buffalo, studied scienza politica at the University of Florence, and earned the Ed.D. degree from Teachers College, Columbia.